**YOU CAN MAKE SOMEONE LOVE YOU . . .
AND *STAY* IN LOVE WITH YOU.**

What you are about to read is the most valuable
information you'll ever receive regarding your love
life. It is so valuable that you should read it several
times, underline it, say it out loud, write it down on a
separate note card, and share it with everyone!

We fall in love with a man or a woman
because of *the way we feel about ourselves*
when we are with them.

DISCOVER HOW TO MAKE THIS KNOWLEDGE
WORK FOR YOU IN . . .

THE 10-SECOND KISS

ALSO BY ELLEN KREIDMAN

Light His Fire
Light Her Fire
Is There Sex After Kids?

The
10
Second
Kiss

ELLEN KREIDMAN, Ph.D.

A Dell Book

Published by
Dell Publishing
a division of
Random House, Inc.
1540 Broadway
New York, New York 10036

ISBN: 978-0-4406-1397-8

Reprinted by arrangement with Renaissance Books

Published simultaneously in Canada

146673257

This book is dedicated to my husband, Steve—
the kindest, most loving, patient, supportive man I know.
Together we have raised three wonderful children who
bring us joy every single day of our lives.
I am more attracted to him and more in love with him
today than when we first fell in love in high school.
I'm so glad we have kept the promise we made at the
altar thirty-one years ago, because I could never have
known this kind of happiness without him.
I love waking up to him every morning and giving him a
ten-second kiss every night.

ACKNOWLEDGMENTS

I am blessed and forever grateful to have the following people in my life:

My parents, who provided me with a secure childhood and an environment where I could reach, stretch, and grow.

Martha Wolf, a mother every daughter dreams of having. Her good nature, compassion, and sense of humor have touched my life in many ways.

My daughter Tara, who brightens every day and gives meaning to my life. Her warmth, generosity, and thoughtfulness remind me how fortunate I am to have her as my daughter. Her insight, feedback, and encouragement early on helped sharpen my thoughts about this book.

My daughter Tiffany, who brings joy and laughter to my life. She reminds me how much fun it is to be a mother. Her unconditional love and constant support have given me added strength when I needed it. Her comments and suggestions helped me clarify many thoughts and ideas on the subject matter for this book.

My son, Jason, who has enriched my life with his love and enthusiasm. His boundless energy, dedication, and compassion fill me with pride. Since he's joined the corporation, his visionary approach, creative thoughts, and insights have provided the fuel necessary to propel my message to a higher level and have given me the freedom to write this book.

My brother Harvey and sister-in-law Susan, who have given me their love and support and have made me a proud aunt to their beautiful children, Matthew and Allison.

My sister-in-law Barbara and her husband, Dale, who gave me an enormous amount of comfort and companionship during some difficult times.

Bill Hartley, "the Chairman of the Universe," an insightful editor who always made suggestions with the utmost tact and improved the manuscript every step of the way. As a supportive publisher, his enthusiasm and belief that I could finish this project on time were contagious. Most importantly, on a personal level, Bill is a kind and compassionate man who has touched my life deeply.

Kathy Dawson, who is a living example of the principles I teach. Her endless hours of dedication, energy, and creative talents were a labor of love. The stories she contributed gave life to my concepts, thoughts, and ideas.

Sandra Caton, whose brilliant and intuitive mind brought focus and clarity to the manuscript.

Jeff Salsberg, CEO of MSI Inc., who exemplifies courage, honesty, and integrity and who believed that my message was worth the risk to produce a TV infomercial to be aired nationwide.

David Bergstrom, president of MSI Inc., whose wisdom, creativity, and sound business sense helped my message reach a wider audience. He taught me that working hard and having fun go hand in hand. With his skillful leadership, determination, and foresight, my dream has become a reality.

Katie McCarthy, executive vice president of MSI Inc., whose excellent direction pushed me to give more than I'd thought I could. Her endless hours of editing, fine-tuning, and creative input are the reason for the success of my infomercials. I marvel at her enthusiasm, decisiveness, and talent.

Andy Foreman, who helped record and package my classes on audiocassette tapes when I first began teaching. His support continues today, as the person responsible for the manufacturing and packaging of my complete product line. What started out as a professional alliance has developed into a wonderful friendship over the years.

Frankie Wright, whose daily encouragement and belief in me over the years has helped spread my message and fill my seminars. As my "chemo buddy," her friendship and devotion played an important part in my healing.

Dr. Neil Barth, my oncologist, who is one of the most remarkable men I'll ever have the pleasure of knowing. He is a true healer in every sense of the word. He is always available, never hurries his patients, gives his undivided attention, answers every question, and projects hope. I have no doubt that I've had the best medical care possible because of a doctor who has a brilliant mind, a positive attitude, and a big heart.

Dr. Barth's office nursing staff—competent, dedicated professionals working tirelessly to make their patients as happy and comfortable as possible. In particular, Kelly Ditmore, R.N., Cheryl Ohlhaver, R.N., Lisa Werkmeister, R.N., Sue Shultes, R.N., and Susann Voyer.

The entire staff of Hoag Cancer Center and Hospital, who believe that the quality of care and the quality of caring are both important health services.

All the men and women who have taken the time to write to me about their experiences and the changes that have occurred as a result of taking my classes, listening to my audiocassette tapes, watching my videos, or attending my seminars. Without their stories this book could not have been written.

CONTENTS

WARNING!!!
DO NOT READ THIS
BOOK UNLESS:

■ You want to have warm, loving, tender feelings toward your mate.

■ You want to experience more passion, excitement, and intimacy with the one you love.

■ You want to continue to have the feelings you had when you first fell in love.

■ You want to feel deeply connected and secure with your mate.

■ You want to have a more satisfying and pleasurable sex life.

I REPEAT: DO NOT UNDER ANY

CIRCUMSTANCES READ THE

FOLLOWING MATERIAL UNLESS YOU

WANT TO EXPERIENCE PASSION,

PLEASURE, AND PLAYFULNESS WITH

THE LOVE OF YOUR LIFE!

PREFACE

I want to thank you in advance for reading this book. I know it's going to cost you quite a bit to do it. I'm not talking about your money. I'm talking about your time. The way I see it, your time is much more valuable than your money will ever be. Do you know why? Because when you spend or lose money, you can always earn more, but when you spend a day, you will always have one less day to spend and you can never get it back. I don't care how influential, educated, good-looking, rich, or poor you are, we all had just twenty-four hours yesterday and we all have only twenty-four hours today

Life is not a dress rehearsal. We don't know how long we're here for. So, since we're not going to get more time, the questions we should all be asking ourselves are, "How can I get more out of the time I have right now?" and, more importantly, "How can I get more out of the time I spend with my mate?"

I don't believe that anything happens by chance. I think that if you saw me on TV or heard me on the radio, if a friend recommended that you read this book, or if it just caught your eye in the bookstore, there is definitely a reason for you to read it.

I believe that this book has been brought to your attention because you are supposed to find out just how easy it is to have fun, romance, communication, and passion in your relationship; how easy it is to turn a boring, ho-hum relationship into a passionate love affair; how easy it is to take a relationship that's on the verge of extinction and bring back the wonderful feelings you had when you first fell in love.

I haven't been called the Fairy Godmother of Relationships for nothing! In just the few short hours it takes to read this book, the magic wand of knowledge will touch your life. As you apply the principles you learn here, you will see immediate results. The changes you seek will not take years, months, or even weeks to achieve. In just twenty-four hours, you can have the relationship you've always dreamed about. You and your mate can become the couple envied by everyone. And when you are finished reading this book, you'll wonder why experts have made this subject seem so complicated, when it is really so simple.

Throughout the book, I will share letters I have received from ordinary people who've had extraordinary results with the principles I teach. I have not changed punctuation, grammar, spelling, or sentence structure because I want you to read the letters as they were written, from the heart. I have changed the names to protect the writers' privacy.

It is my hope that the next letter I get is from you, letting me know the changes that have taken place in your relationship as a result of putting what you read in these pages into action.

The
10
Second
Kiss

INTRODUCTION

This Can't Be Happening to Me

When I heard the surgeon's words, my first thought was, "No. He's wrong. This can't be happening to me." Grasping for straws, I thought maybe I had misunderstood.

But I knew I hadn't. I knew he really had said, "I'm so sorry, honey. It's cancer."

Uncontrollable panic seized me as the words began to sink in. I couldn't breathe and my chest hurt so badly I felt like I had been run over by a truck. The blood drained from my head and I was afraid I was going to pass out in my chair. It seemed utterly impossible that only moments ago I had been joking and laughing with the doctor, confident that the biopsy was a waste of time and money.

"Oh, God," I cried. "Please say this isn't true! What am I going to tell Steve?"

My husband was in the outer waiting room engrossed in conversation with a stranger, oblivious to the terror that gripped me. How was I going to tell him, the man I had loved since I was a teenager, that I had just heard what felt like my death sentence?

My Love Story

Steve and I met in high school and quickly fell in love. I was sixteen and in my junior year, and he was seventeen and a senior. We were quite a team, spending just about every waking moment together. I helped him with his English homework and he helped me get through math. Our parents thought we were too young to be so serious about each other, so we listened to them and ended up separating and going to different colleges. Although we both dated other people in college, neither of us ever met anyone who could even come close to evoking the feelings we had for each other. So in our senior year we got engaged, and we were married soon after graduation.

In the years that followed, our life together had been good, but far from perfect—better than many, perhaps, but we'd had our share of hard times. We had experienced bankruptcy, tragedy, disappointment, and loss, but never had we faced a life-threatening illness.

Now here it was 1991, and I was on top of the world. Both of my books, *Light His Fire* and *Light Her Fire*, had become *New York Times* best-sellers. I was in demand as a TV talk-show guest and was earning top dollar on the lecture circuit. Then, at the height of my career, my world was turned upside down. One day I was living a dream life, and the next day I was starring in a nightmare that wouldn't go away. I was forty-seven years old and, because the cancer was in an advanced stage and had spread to several of my lymph nodes, I had only a 30 percent chance of survival. I was facing a mastectomy, followed by months of chemotherapy, and was told that I would be lucky to come out of it alive.

The surgery took place the following day. There was no time to waste and no time to get used to the idea that I was losing a breast. Under the circumstances, it wasn't too difficult to convince myself that it was a fair trade—a breast for my life. After a rather shaky recuperation, with some setbacks that necessitated a return to the hospital, I was ready for the next step—chemotherapy.

More Than a Statistic

My husband and I began the search for an oncologist to whom we could entrust my life. We interviewed half a dozen doctors who gave me a poor prognosis and very little hope for survival before we finally found one who gave us hope. When we asked Dr. Neil Barth of Newport Beach, California, what my chances of survival were he replied, "A powerful will to live is much more important than a numerical survival rate," and we knew our search was over. I feel so fortunate to have found a doctor who believed I was more than a statistic. Even if I were to die, I didn't want the time I had left to be a negative, hopeless experience. I am convinced that the reason I did so well with my treatment was largely because I had a doctor who was very positive and supportive in his approach.

When I started chemotherapy, I managed to ignore my fears during the day as long as I kept busy. But at night, I'd have a difficult time. I'd wake up often, and in the silence of the night my thoughts would terrify me. Steve would try to comfort me, holding me in his arms and stroking me, as we both cried ourselves back to sleep. I desperately needed a way to turn off the voice in my head that kept scaring me with dark thoughts.

Miraculously, just as I reached total exhaustion from lack of sleep and was sure I would never again sleep in peace, a package arrived in the mail. It was a box of audiotapes, sent by a man I knew only from a couple of telephone conversations. Bill Hartley, who had published a condensed version of my audiocassette programs, had heard about my diagnosis and decided to send me some self-help tapes. They were the best the mind-body field had to offer, and included the thoughts of Dr. Bernie Siegel, Dr. Carl Simonton, and Dr. Paul Pearsall. These inspirational voices became my constant companions, and as I'd lie in bed at night, listening to the tapes over and over again, I began to feel hope instead of despair and was finally able to sleep. Later, when I had the strength, I wrote to Bill to tell him the impact those tapes had on my life and to thank him for this loving act of kindness from a virtual stranger. At that time, neither of us had an inkling that one day he would be the publisher of this, my fourth book.

A Reason to Celebrate

Over the next year, I completely altered my life-style. My desire to live was so strong that I was willing to do anything that would give me a better chance. Once I had completed all of the chemotherapy and other treatments prescribed by the medical profession, I became an expert on healthy diet and habits. Following a strict regime of proper diet, exercise, and daily prayers of gratitude, I grew healthier every day. In fact, I had never felt better, and in 1992 I wrote *How Can We Light a Fire When the Kids Are Driving Us Crazy?* It was published the following year and was retitled *Is There Sex After Kids?* when it was later released in paperback. It shows parents how to be lovers too. Steve and I were closer than ever, our three beautiful children continued to grow and prosper, and life was beginning to feel normal again.

Two years later, Steve and I were vacationing in Hawaii, enjoying life, and celebrating three and a half years cancer-free. I remember standing on the balcony of our hotel room, which overlooked the beautiful blue water of the Pacific Ocean, and feeling the soft warm breeze on my face. Suddenly I was overcome with gratitude for the preciousness of that moment. I looked up to the sky and said, "God, thank you so much for restoring my health. I feel so lucky to be alive." I had no idea at the time that my world would soon come crashing down on me again.

A Fight for Survival

Shortly after our return, in February 1995, a routine six-month checkup revealed another lump. Further tests confirmed a recurrence of breast cancer. My oncologist felt that my only chance for survival was a bone marrow transplant. "No. Oh, no," I whispered, tears streaming down my face. "This can't be happening again!"

When I got home, all I could do was scream, "Oh God, what did I do to deserve this?" over and over again. My fear had turned to rage, and it was a long time before I could let God into my life again.

Was this the end? Was I going to die from this disease? I was heartsick to think I might not get to see my kids marry and have children. It was unthinkable that my life with my husband might be over. How could he cope without me there by his side? We'd been inseparable forever! I desperately wanted to live.

My first bout with cancer had taken so much out of me. I was terrified that my fifty-year-old body, which had been through so much already, couldn't survive another assault on it—one that would be even more deadly than the first had been. There were practical considerations too. For a while it was questionable whether our medical insurance would pay for the procedure. Much negotiating took place before we were finally assured that it would be covered.

Before the transplant could take place, I had to endure more drugs and endless rounds of chemotherapy. My own bone marrow was to be harvested in advance of the procedure. It was no piece of cake, believe me, but this time I already knew how hard it is to stay focused on healing when your body is so battered and wasted. Determined to prepare mentally for my own personal World War II, I armed myself with every book and audiocassette available that had anything to do with healing the mind and body. Louise L. Hay, Dr. Deepak Chopra, Dr. Wayne W. Dyer, and dozens of other experts filled my mind with positive thoughts and the belief that I could get through this. After I got over my initial rage, I also had many conversations with God and knew that He would be with me every step of the way. Being a strong believer in the power of prayer, whenever anyone asked what they could do for me, I always responded, "Pray."

A Reason to Live

In June 1995, I entered Hoag Hospital in Newport Beach, California, for my bone marrow transplant. I'll always be grateful to my daughter's boss for the best "get well" gift I could have received. She had arranged for a family photo, taken during happier times, to be blown up to poster size, and she sent it to me just before I went into the hospital. I took that beautiful poster to the hospital with me and hung it on the wall at the foot of my bed. Seeing that picture of my husband and children smiling down at me every time I opened my eyes was a constant reminder of my reasons for living.

During the time that I was in the hospital, I anticipated my husband's daily visits and his tender kiss of greeting with the hunger of a starving person. His kisses had such a powerful, healing impact on me. No matter how sick or weak I was, his kisses always breathed new life into me. They were so sweet, so gentle, always reminding me of how much I was loved. There I was—no hair, no eyebrows, no eyelashes—hooked up to life support and feeling ugly, useless, and helpless, and he still wanted to kiss me! What an affirmation of love. I just had to gain back my strength so I could love him back in the same way.

And I did! With the help of a brilliant doctor and a team of dedicated nurses, the love of my devoted husband and children, and the powerful prayers of friends both near and far, I can again celebrate being cancer-free.

Being of Most Benefit

When I was first diagnosed with cancer, I prayed for a miracle. Now I realize that every day is a miracle. Having to face my own mortality has made me realize what a fragile and unpredictable gift life is and how lucky I am to be here to enjoy it. It also strengthened my conviction that love is truly the only thing that matters. I believe it is the main reason we are put on this earth.

I also remember promising God that if He granted me a miracle and I survived, I would dedicate the rest of my life to sharing with as many people as I could the joy of giving and receiving love. Never underestimate the power of prayer! One day out of the blue, about six months after my transplant, I received a phone call from MSI Inc. asking me to do an infomercial. It would be a thirty-minute interview in which I would explain the benefits of my audiocassette programs, *Light His Fire, Light Her Fire,* and *Light Your Fire.* I agreed, never dreaming that I would touch so many lives as a result. To date, over one million of these programs have been sold. The way I see it, so many people prayed for me that God must have said, "Okay, I'll give her good health, let her help people with their relationships, and I'll throw in a little money as well." I feel so blessed to have a career that I am so passionate about and the strength to be able to create these life-changing programs.

Too Late or Just in Time

I receive an incredible amount of mail from all over the United States and from many other countries as well. Most of the letters fall into two categories: those letting me know that the writer found out about my programs too late to benefit from them, and those thanking me for the help they've received.

For those who ask, "Where were you one, two, or three years ago when I really needed you?" I feel their pain and frustration. It is very upsetting to know that my help wasn't available to save their past relationship, but I do know that they now have the information they need to make their next one work. Many even admit that they never would have listened to me if they hadn't first gone through the pain of losing the one they loved.

I received one such letter from Joe, a man who simply didn't get the information in time.

I've just finished listening to your audiocassette program, Light Her Fire, *which I thoroughly enjoyed, but it made me sick. Let me explain. Almost everything you say to do, I did the opposite. What a jerk I've been. I just sent for your tapes to try to find out why my relationships just don't work for the long haul. I'm forty-six years old, have a good job, am active in sports, a good dancer and women say I'm nice looking and have a good sense of humor. I've been married twice and both times my wives left me for other men! What's wrong with me? Well, now I know at least some of the reasons why my last marriage didn't work. Here are just a few reasons.*

I didn't do the little things, like call her during the day to see how she was doing and to tell her how much I loved her. I didn't bring flowers home once in a while or get her a card when it wasn't a special occasion. I never made a big deal about her birthday or anniversaries. It was always a pain to go out and get something. I always got the first thing I came across, and she knew it. I did not put her first in my life. My friends and my job came before her. I always looked like a slob on the weekends. I never shaved or wore anything nice. Since I shaved every day for work, I figured it wasn't necessary. Wrong!! And last but not least, we had sex, we never made love. I was very selfish and when I got what I wanted, I was finished. I'm surprised they stayed with me as long as they did.

But you've taught me what I need to do. The next woman I go out with is going to be really lucky to have found me. I'm going to treat her right and keep treating her right. I don't want to end up alone. I want to make someone feel special and feel loved myself. Thank you for showing me the way.

The other kind of letters I receive, the letters of gratitude, are filled with excitement and wonderful testimonials of changed lives. They are nothing short of miraculous.

Here is a letter from Jeannie, which proves that it's never too late to fall in love all over again.

A little over a month ago, my husband and I (married thirteen years) had decided to call it quits. It had always been said by family and friends that we had the perfect marriage. However, the truth was . . . we were simply pretending to be who everyone else perceived us to be. We were great actors!

The day after we seriously discussed a divorce, I saw a brief portion of your interview on cable with Peter Tomarken. I called my husband into the room and said, "Listen to this." When it was over, we agreed to order your program, Light Her Fire *and* Light His Fire. *I felt hope for the first time in several years. I knew at that moment that my husband still cared enough to try . . . that he still loved me and I still loved him.*

Luckily, your program arrived in just a couple of weeks. Although we have not yet completed your program, I had to take a moment and write this letter. In just a little over a week, my marriage of thirteen years has been transformed. The change was almost instantaneous. Just the other night (one of our date nights) at a restaurant, he reached across the table, took my hand in his, and through tears he said, "I just want you to know how much you mean to me and how much I love you." Just as you say on the tapes, it didn't matter that something in your program might have prompted him to say it . . . he said it!!! Before I leave for work each morning, I hear "I love you" or "you sure do *look pretty this morning" instead of "leave me the check-book" or "have you got a $5 bill?" Just like an excited little boy, he grabs a tape each morning and each day I anticipate what will happen as a result.*

In just a few days, I have already sent him flowers at his office (which also made him cry), left him dirty (love) messages on his voice mail at work, paid him a different compliment each and every day, and tonight (a Tuesday night) my mom is keeping our little girl just so that we can have dinner and a night alone. I can't wait!

Now you know why I never listen when someone tells me they are on the verge of divorce.

Here is another letter that proves that no matter how bad you think things are, there is always hope.

I just can't tell you how much your tapes have helped me. They have changed my whole life. I've learned so much about relationships. Let me tell you a little about myself. I'm twenty-five years old with three kids, a six-year-old girl, a four-year-old boy and we recently adopted my thirteen-year-old niece. We've been married six years and we were almost going to get a divorce. Things seemed so hopeless and not worth the effort. He was cold and selfish and there was no romance in our marriage at all. My birthday would just come and go. We'd even fight on my birthday because I would always be so hurt that he didn't even acknowledge it was my day. Well, I've come a long way since then. I feel as though the shields have been lifted from my eyes. It feels so great!! I follow your tapes step by step, doing everything you say, and it works. Not only do I feel like I'm a happier person, but my marriage is better than ever. I'm not so stressed all the time and like you said, my love cup is full all the time now. Ellen, there is so much to tell you, but I don't think you have time to read a book right now. I do have one story to tell you from the cassette Romance Is a Decision. *Well, I put something sexy on and lit a few candles with soft music in the background and I sprayed some of my perfume in the room. (By the way I sent all the kids to my dad's house.) My husband was in the shower while I did all this so when he came into the room his eyes almost popped out of their sockets. Boy, was he ready. . . . I just had to thank you for your help. When the last tape was over, I felt like a friendship had ended. I have to say I miss talking to you.*

Thank you with all the sincerity in the world. By the way, the night my husband and I made passionate love by candlelight, we made a baby. I'm pregnant. Beautiful things can happen.

The following letter from Michael shows that persistence can pay off.

I must write to you to let you know your information on the Light Her Fire *tapes has saved my marriage and kept my family together. We had been separated for a year. I had tried everything I knew without success. I got the tapes and started telling her all the things I know and felt but rarely said. Keep in mind that we were headed for our final court hearing to end our marriage. I just started to hug and hold her and tell her that she meant more to me than anything or anybody. She would tell me to stop, but I would listen to you, not her.*

About a month or two after I started listening and doing what you said to do, I got a call one night that blew me away. She calls me and says she wants to see me. Keep in mind that this is the woman that would not go to coffee, dinner, or a movie and said she never would.

Well, we not only have been out to dinner and a movie, but our sex life has been better than it's ever been in the thirteen years we have known each other.

After a time when it seemed things were going well, I gave her the Light His Fire *tapes, which she is listening to as well.*

I know as a woman you want all the details, but being a man, I must be brief.

Who says a woman can't be brief? This letter from Linda was short and sweet.

I recently ordered your Light His Fire/Light Her Fire *tapes, and I must tell you that after listening to only the first tape, my husband and I had a honeymoon night as if we were twenty-year-old newlyweds. We have been married for about fifteen years (second marriage for both) and I thought that my lack of sexual interest was due to the onset of menopause (forty-seven years old). This, however, is not so, and you have proven it. I am familiar with the principles you speak about throughout the tapes, but unfortunately, I never integrated them into a daily routine. Your tapes have reminded me to constantly be aware of these guidelines and principles. To apply them often means to make a difference for people who matter in my life. You are truly a genius in the field of human relations. Thank you, thank you, thank you.*

The following letter always brings tears to my eyes. Hal reminds us all that we never know how much time we have left to love our mate the way they deserve to be loved.

I was divorced in June and bought your program one month later. I started listening to your tapes and they were working. I was back living with my wife, even though she hadn't listened to her set yet. Then on August 24th, she drowned in a river near Cody, Wyoming. I want to thank you so much for the tapes. If my wife had not drowned we would have been married again. I know now that our lives would have been better than before because of your program. After she passed away I found out that she was planning a trip for two to Tahiti. Thank you for the little time we had together before she passed away.

Planting a Seed

Many of the people who have been affected by attending my seminars or listening to my audiocassette programs have expressed an interest in teaching my course so that they too could have an impact on people's lives. As a result, I developed a course for potential teachers, and today classes are being taught throughout the U.S. and in other parts of the world. The knowledge that I can duplicate what I teach through other people has given me a great deal of pride and joy. One letter that is especially precious to me was sent by Kathy, an instructor who teaches my programs in Cleveland, Ohio. She wrote this letter at three o'clock on the morning she was scheduled to have surgery. I still get emotional every time I read it. She wrote:

I have every intention of getting through this surgery, but just in case, I want you to know what a difference you've made in my life and the lives of those around me. I have enjoyed these last four years of teaching your program more than any other years in my life, and it's because of you.

I'll never forget the day I dropped to my knees in our walk-in closet and broke into sobs. I had been married five years and had two children, both in diapers. I loved my husband and children, but my life had become mundane and robotic. I wanted meaning and passion back in my marriage and in my life.

I remember praying on my knees in our closet, "God, please guide me. I can't do this by myself. I have so much more to give in my life and to give to my husband. But I don't know how. I need your help."

I got help that following Christmas when my husband bought me your book, Light His Fire. *After reading your book, I started doing loving things in our relationship, even though I didn't feel like it. What I felt like was a cow that everyone was sucking off of, but I pretended to feel energized and attractive.*

Within the first few weeks of behaving differently toward my husband, he started to respond in the same loving way. By the end of two weeks, I felt like I really mattered to him. BINGO! Life was meaningful again.

I remember tracking you down while you were in Cleveland on a book tour, convinced that I was supposed to teach your course in my hometown. When you said you would train me to become a teacher, you planted a seed that has spread through thousands and thousands of lives.

It has been my privilege to help you do that. I met people I never would have met and loved in a way I never would have loved.

You are truly a vehicle through whom God has worked and will continue to work for many years to come. My life has been blessed by knowing you.

I love you. Kathy

I am happy to report that Kathy made it through her surgery and is still teaching classes in Cleveland.

Now, I know that not everyone wants to teach classes or give lectures, but I also know that every one of you reading this book will have the opportunity to touch someone's life in some way. That's the reason I've written it.

For those of you who have not read *Light His Fire, Light Her Fire,* or *Is There Sex After Kids?,* don't worry. We'll start off together from here. Those of you who have read my other books or listened to my programs will recognize some of the life-changing concepts that I've presented in the past. The purpose of this book, however, is to take you to a new level of awareness. After all, many years have passed since I first began teaching these concepts, and during that time I have experienced, learned, taught, and seen a great deal that I want to pass on to you.

There is so much comfort, romance, and fun in a relationship where you are never too busy to be there for each other. Like my husband and I, you too can experience a love that is so deep and complete that no crisis will ever tear you apart. Using the concepts in this book, you and your mate can be lovers, not for just a few months or those brief youthful years, but for life. In the following chapters, we will intensify your resolve, stretch your imagination, and explore more possibilities than you ever dreamed possible.

Your relationship is the most important aspect of your life. To **K**eep **I**t **S**omething **S**pecial (K.I.S.S.) follow the K.I.S.S. Plan at the end of each chapter. This is where you'll get specific instructions on how to put into practice what you've just learned. Remember: as in any worthwhile undertaking, to get results you must do the exercises. Yes, it will take time and effort on your part, but the effort will pay off with a more loving, understanding, and passionate mate . . . one who will always be there for you.

1
THE
TEN-SECOND
KISS

The Magical Countdown

*W*hen a couple stands at the altar and vows to love each other "till death do us part," they take for granted that they will stay intimately connected forever. The kiss at the end of the ceremony is symbolic of that connection, and throughout the relationship the kiss remains at the core. The kiss is the most intimate connection possible between two people—even more intimate than sexual intercourse, as I'll explain later in this chapter.

Sadly, as the years pass, staying connected with our mate gradually takes a back seat to all the mundane duties and chores that exist in a marriage. In reality, everything else should take a back seat to our love for each other.

Jennifer and Ron could not remember when their relationship changed. All they knew was with two young children, two careers, and too little time, their marriage was in jeopardy. They had become working partners instead of loving partners. It was their thirteenth anniversary and Jennifer's mother had offered to baby-sit so they could have a special weekend, but instead of a romantic resort they chose to come to my lecture, hoping for a miracle.

I had asked for a volunteer couple from the audience to tell me what they believed was the biggest problem in their relationship. Jennifer and Ron came up on the stage at my urging and began to explain. "We have no time for each other. We're both so busy that at the end of the day, we just give each other a quick peck on the cheek, mumble good night, and we're off to sleep," said Jennifer. "Sometimes—often, actually—we don't even bother with the kiss."

Egging them on a little, I asked Ron how it was that they couldn't find the time to invest in the most important aspect of their lives.

"Well," he responded, "we both have demanding jobs, which sometimes require travel away from home. Jennifer travels more than I do, at least once a month, but when I'm gone it's for a longer period of time. Usually a week or two. And, of course, there're the kids. They have to be driven to school each morning and picked up from day-care each evening. Then there's grocery shopping, meal preparation and cleanup—Jennifer does that while I help the kids with their homework. You wouldn't believe how much homework kids are given these days. After dinner and homework are over, we try to spend some quality time with the kids before we put them to bed. When one of us is gone on a business trip, it all falls on the other's shoulders."

"On the weekends," Jennifer piped in, "we have the house to clean, the yard to tend, errands to run, home-repair chores, shopping for clothes and school supplies for the kids, and Ron's parents are elderly, so they require some of our time too. And, we do try to keep up some semblance of a social life, but it isn't easy."

I replied that I could see they were certainly very busy people. Then I asked them, "Do you think you could find just ten seconds in your busy day to devote to your relationship?"

At first they just laughed. They thought I was joking. When they realized it was a serious question, they both replied "yes" in unison.

At this point, I turned to the five thousand people seated in the auditorium and, gesturing with my hands, I asked them all to stand up. Anxious for a stretch break, they complied willingly. But when I said, "Now, I want you all to face your partner and give him or her a ten-second kiss," there was an uproar of groans and sighs. Ignoring it, I added, "I'm going to time you, so no cheating or letting up before I say 'stop'!" Somebody in the crowd asked, "Do we have to?" in a loud voice.

"Come on," I said. "You can do it. This is not torture. It will be fun and it's part of the lecture. Yes, you have to do it!"

This part of my lecture usually takes more time than I'd like, but I always stand my ground and continue to coax them until every single person is ready to participate. Then the magical ten-second countdown begins as they start to kiss: One thousand and one, one thousand and two, one thousand and three, one thousand and four, on up to one thousand and ten, and then . . . "STOP!"

The crowd was wild with enthusiasm as I directed them back to their seats. I could actually feel the mood of the entire room change. It was filled with excitement, warmth, and electricity. "Now, that wasn't so awful, was it?" I asked, smiling. Loud clapping, whistling, and cheering signaled their approval. Turning to Jennifer and Ron, I asked them what the ten-second kiss had been like for them.

"I was really uncomfortable," Jennifer replied. "Not just because of being in front of so many people. We just aren't in the habit of kissing like that anymore, except when we make love. But I think I could get used to it," she added with a laugh.

Thanking them for their openness and courage for coming up on stage, I told them they could return to their seats.

The Connection

Then I went on to explain to the audience that sometimes what starts out as a passionate relationship, over time, winds up as a friendship. We are so caught up in our daily routine that we forget all about keeping closeness and passion alive. Many times we're not even aware that this change has occurred, but one day we wake up and realize with a shock that we are living as roommates instead of lovers.

Living with a good friend means there's mutual

respect, common interests, companionship, and security, but no passion. It may not be the worst thing that can happen, but I'm here to tell you that you can keep your best friend and get your lover back too.

Engaging in a ten-second kiss every day declares that you are lovers—not just roommates. It helps you stay connected. Even though you may tell your mate you love them every day, giving them a ten-second kiss tells them, "I'm still in love with you."

The ten-second kiss has a more immediate and dramatic effect on a relationship than any other homework I've ever assigned. Given in the morning, it sets the tone for the rest of the day. Given early in the evening, it sets the mood for the rest of the night. No matter what time of day you kiss, you'll feel warm, close, and connected. The casual kiss, the peck on the cheek are ways of saying our relationship is comfortable, platonic. In order to go from pleasant to passionate, you have to feel how delicious and meaningful a ten-second kiss really is.

I use this exercise in all of my seminars because I want to demonstrate to people that it doesn't matter whether they feel like kissing each other or not: the result of the ten-second kiss is the same. They may feel distant, annoyed, embarrassed, humiliated, or uncomfortable before the kiss. But when they do it anyway, the result of their action is a feeling of connection, warmth, safety, tenderness, and even passion. Usually, the ones who resist it the most are the ones who enjoy it so much they refuse to stop even when the time is up.

Act "As If"

Some of us believe that we must feel a certain way before we can act a certain way. As one procrastinator I know is fond of saying, "I'm waiting for the spirit to move me." Quite frankly, if I waited to do things until I felt like it, I'd never do anything!

I am proposing a different point of view: **You can create love every day by acting in a loving way and not worrying about whether you are feeling loving!**

How many times have you said, "I'm not in the mood to . . . ," "I don't want to . . . ," or "I don't feel like it . . . ," then not done whatever it was and as a result felt badly all day?

For example, I do not like to exercise. Given a chance, I'd much rather read. I know, however, that exercise is good for me, and now that I'm older, I really feel that it's important for me to engage in some form of exercise every day. But each morning when I wake up my first thought is always, "I'm not in the mood today," "It's too hot," or "It's too cold." Never do I wake up and think, "Oh, goody. I get to exercise now." Still, I get up, brush my teeth, comb my hair, put on my walking shoes and my warm-up suit, and begin exercising anyway. Ten minutes of stretching, ten minutes of floor exercises, and a brisk one-mile walk every day, rain or shine, tired or not. The amazing thing about this ritual is that, no matter how I felt before I exercised, I always feel great afterward. I'm proud of myself and I'm energized and ready to face the day.

Here's the point. If I waited until I was in the mood, I'd stay in bed all day, because that's what I feel like doing when I wake up every morning. Can you imagine how miserable I'd be if I acted on how I felt, instead of what I knew was good for me?

Here's another example. I don't want to clean my house. I hate housework. I've done it for so long. What's the expression? "Been there, done that!" But I've learned that if I simply begin to clean, even though I'm thinking, "I'd rather be at the beach" or "Someday I'll get live-in help!" nevertheless I'm soon done, I feel a sense of accomplishment, and I'm in a better mood.

Believe it or not, shopping is right up there with housecleaning on my list of things I don't like to do. Since I've been involved in so many creative projects—writing, speaking engagements, and television appearances—I don't even like to shop for clothes anymore. And I've never been fond of grocery shopping. But if I waited until I was in the mood, I'd probably be naked and starving to death! So regardless of how I feel, I do buy a new outfit for a television appearance or a speaking engagement and I do go to the supermarket for my weekly groceries. And although I may not want to at the time, I'm sure glad I did when I open my refrigerator and see food in there.

I'm not saying we shouldn't be in touch with our feelings, but it's often possible to change our feelings by changing our actions. I remember when I first began teaching my classes, I decided to participate in Orange County's first Women's Conference. I presented two seminars during the day, and rented exhibit space to promote my classes.

Finished with my afternoon presentation, I was packing up all of my materials when the program coordinator spotted me as she walked out of the main ballroom. She approached me, and in a desperate voice said, "Ellen, I'm so glad you're still here. We have a problem. Our keynote speaker hasn't shown up and we have a thousand people expecting to hear a presentation. Would you take her place?"

Dumbfounded, I said, "Are you crazy? You scheduled the most popular newscaster in the city as the keynote speaker. People are waiting to hear about her life and accomplishments. I'd stand up for forty-five minutes and talk about relationships!"

Beginning to panic, I looked around to find that all the other presenters had packed up their materials and were already inside the ballroom waiting for the closing speech. At that moment, I felt like running out the nearest exit and never looking back. But instead I heard myself say, "Okay. I guess I can do it."

When I stepped up to the podium, I looked into the sea of faces and felt sheer terror. I was used to speaking to a group of twenty-five students. There were over one thousand women out there. My hands trembled as I adjusted the microphone and my voice cracked as I said, "I'm not the person you came to hear today . . ."

I went on to tell them of my background and ways they could improve their relationships. As I made my points and shared anecdotes, I was energized by the enthusiasm and laughter from the audience. By the end of the forty-five minutes, I was loving it. Evidently, the audience was too, because they gave me a standing ovation.

For the first time, I realized I could speak in front of a large group. But I would never have found out if

I had given in to my fear. By accepting the challenge in spite of my insecurity, I gained the confidence I needed to expand my horizons and bring my message to other large groups.

Whether it's exercising, cleaning the house, or doing the filing, I'm sure you can think of something you don't feel like doing, but once you've done it, you're glad you did.

Try It, You'll Like It

The year I was forty my children decided they wanted to go skiing for our family vacation. Since children are the best salespeople in the world, they persuaded my husband that learning to ski would be great fun for all of us. I wasn't so convinced. My husband's choice of where to ski didn't boost my confidence either. Instead of choosing a nice resort with beginners' slopes, he led us to a challenging mountain in Utah. I remember him saying, "If we're going to do this, we're going to do it right."

I had never skied in my life and I was petrified. "Ellen," I said to myself, "if you are crazy enough to go up that mountain on a chairlift, suspended hundreds of feet above the ground, and then come down it on two long skinny slats with nothing to stop you but a tree, you will wind up a paraplegic for the rest of your life. You will never walk or talk again. You are too old to learn to ski!"

I definitely did not feel like going skiing but I went anyway. I did not feel like taking a ski lesson, but I did it anyway. And do you know what? By the end of the vacation, I could ski; not well, but I could ski. And I was very proud that I had decided to go in spite of my fear.

Many of you do not feel like getting up for work when the alarm rings in the morning. Your first thoughts may be, "Oh no, is it time to get up already?" or "I'm so tired," or "Maybe I'll call in sick today," or "I don't want to get up!" But you do it anyway, and at the end of the day, you feel productive and glad you've earned another paycheck. It's the doing that makes us feel good. So when you read an assignment in this book and you don't feel like doing it—do it anyway! Trust me when I say that you'll be glad you did.

No Excuses Please

Whenever I'm teaching a seminar and I introduce new information to people, I know I'm going to hear a lot of excuses. I've spoken to thousands of people in my career, and I think I've heard every excuse in the book. "Sure Ellen, it's easy for you, but . . ." "You can do it, but . . ." "It sounds like a good idea, but . . ." BUT, BUT, BUT, BUT! Okay, let's get the "but"'s out of the way right now. Below are just ten examples from the hundreds of excuses for not giving your mate a ten-second kiss that I've heard over the years. I'll bet yours is here, too.

- Excuse #1: I'd like to give my wife a ten-second kiss when I get home, but I'm afraid my breath will smell and she'll be offended.

■ *Solution: Invest in fifty-two rolls of breath mints, one for each week of the year.*

Howard takes clients to lunch every day, and invariably he'll eat something with garlic in it. "When I tried to kiss my wife after I came home, she'd recoil and say, 'Howard, not now, your breath.' I felt so rejected that I just stayed away from her," he said. "It wasn't until taking *Light Her Fire* that I realized how important that kiss was, so I started keeping a stash of mints in my glove compartment. Now I've got my confidence and my wife back!"

■ Excuse #2: I want to give my husband a ten-second kiss when he gets home, but I can't kiss and keep time all at once.
■ *Solution: Set the microwave or oven timer until you get a feel for how long ten seconds is. If you go over ten seconds . . . oh, well!*

Anita remembers the first time she tried the ten-second kiss on her husband. "I was concentrating so hard on keeping my lips pressed to his for ten seconds that I ended up counting out loud while we were kissing. I remember Al stepping back from me and saying, 'Honey, if you want to tell me something, you can wait until we're done kissing.' "

Anita tried setting an egg timer to get a feel for how long she and her husband should kiss. She and Al got so deeply into the kiss that they didn't even hear the ding. Now their internal clock keeps time for them!

- Excuse #3: I want to give my wife a ten-second kiss when she gets home, but our kids keep coming between us.
- *Solution: Let them try. What better childhood memory could they have than trying to squeeze between Mommy and Daddy while they were kissing.*

When Jane and Tom first practiced a ten-second kiss, they had one major distraction—their daughter. Every time Jane and Tom's lips would meet, their five-year-old daughter, Meagan, would run to them and try to wedge herself between their bodies.

"I could handle feeling her tiny body between our legs," said Tom. "But it was when I felt a Barbie doll shoved into my groin that I decided enough was enough."

Tom and Jane decided the answer to their problem was to use Meagan as their timer. They told her that as soon as she saw her Daddy walk into the room, it was her job to go sit on the couch and count to ten slowly until Daddy and Mommy were done kissing. It worked! Jane and Tom got their ten-second kiss and Meagan didn't feel left out.

Many couples have asked if it was appropriate to kiss in front of their children. Children have no business being in the bedroom, true, but being spectators of a loving kiss? You bet! Heidi told me that when she and her husband first started the ten-second kiss, her eight-year-old son used to squinch up his face and proclaim, "Gross!! Yech!! That's disgusting!" Three years later, at age eleven, he now steps in for a closer look, cranes his neck, and says, "How do you breathe?"

Whether your children come from a "grossed out" perspective or an analytical one, the image of their parents kissing will stay embedded in their memory forever. What a wonderful gift to give to your children!

- Excuse #4: I'd like to give my husband a ten-second kiss when he gets home, but either the phone rings or I'm already talking to someone on it and can't clear my mind of our conversation when I hang up.
- *Solution: Let it ring. Whoever it is can call back or leave a message on your answering machine. If you're on the phone, tell whoever you're talking to that your husband just walked in and you want to finish your conversation later. Your husband will get the message that he matters more to you than whoever was on the other end of the phone.*

Natalie owned a home-based business and was often talking on the phone with a client when her husband came in from work. As soon as she heard the garage door open, she would end the call. Unfortunately, she couldn't turn her thoughts off as easily as she could hang up the phone. As a result, when she was giving her husband a ten-second kiss, she was still thinking about work.

One of the things Natalie loved about working from her home was that there was no time wasted commuting to the office. But she eventually realized that commuting time does have its advantages. It helps us shift gears from the professional mind-set to the personal mind-set. So she decided to create her own "mini-commute." Now, fifteen minutes before her husband is due home, she clears her office, makes a quick reminder list for the day, turns off the ringer on her business line, and lets any late calls go directly to voice mail. Then she actually leaves the house to run an errand, walk the dog, or do some other mindless task. That's her commute, and it helps her make the transition from worktime to playtime. Just a fifteen-minute break and she returns home in a completely new frame of mind—ready to give her husband a ten-second kiss.

- Excuse #5: I'd like to give my wife a ten-second kiss, but the dog is all over me as soon as I open the door.
- *Solution: Don't you dare pet your dog before you kiss your wife. Block out the barking, panting, and sniffing and go for the kiss.*

Mary Lynn writes, "I love dogs just as much as the next guy, but after owning our golden retriever for five years, I began to resent the animal. I'm embarrassed to admit this, but I was jealous of our pet!

"From the day we brought our dog home, my husband developed a routine of stroking him, hugging him, and cooing, 'How's my Petie-pooh today?' whenever he returned home. I believe animals have feelings and need attention, but this was ridiculous.

"After Larry's five-minute ritual with the dog, I'd get a quick glance and a 'Hi, how are ya?' before he would look at the mail. I used to daydream about driving the dog to the country and accidentally hitting the trunk release in our van so the dog would jump out.

"My husband started listening to your tapes and one day when he came home he blew me away. Hearing his car pull into the driveway, I stuck my head in the refrigerator and began reorganizing it so I wouldn't have to witness his daily reunion with our dog. Suddenly, I felt someone grab my waist and spin me around. Before I had a chance to say anything, my husband gave me a kiss so passionate that I forgot I had a jar in my hand and accidentally poured pickle juice down the back of his shirt.

"Since then, we've made a promise to each other. He'll kiss me before he greets our dog, if I kiss him back with free hands. It's been a deal!"

- Excuse #6: I'd like to give my wife a ten-second kiss, but when I come through the door at the end of the day, she hits me with a million problems at once. I can't get her to stop talking long enough to kiss me.
- *Solution: Don't come in the same door every day. Come in another entrance and kiss her. She'll be so surprised that she won't have a chance to start talking.*

Whenever David walked through the door at the end of the day, his wife presented him with some problem he was expected to solve. The gas grill wouldn't work, the computer screen was frozen, or the sliding shower door had fallen off.

"I solve problems all day at work," David told me.

"I don't want to do it at home too, at least not when I first walk through the door."

To avoid being ambushed, he decided to sneak in the house through the side door. Instead of coming in the front hallway, he came through the kitchen. That way he was able to grab Jackie, being careful not to scare her, and give her a long, luscious kiss.

"We have four entrances to our house," said David. "She never knows which one I'm going to use."

David's wife still talks about the problems of the day, but after a ten-second kiss, David feels more like her intimate partner than a dumping ground for problems.

- Excuse #7: I'd like to give my husband a ten-second kiss, but he seems so tense from his day. I don't want to bother him.
- *Solution: The loving energy you'll transfer to him through your kiss will do more to relax him and make him feel cherished than any whirlpool or masseuse.*

Mary used to work herself into a tizzy every day anticipating her husband's return from work. "He was always wound up as tight as a rubber band," said Mary. "I wanted to help him relax, but I never knew how."

When she heard about the ten-second kiss in class, Mary thought it was worth a try, but was skeptical about whether her husband could unwind in just ten seconds. She proved herself wrong. "I remember the first time I tried it. By the time the ten seconds had ended, it felt like Paul had melted in my arms. He tells me it's the best relaxation therapy he's ever had."

- Excuse #8: I want to give my husband a ten-second kiss, but he goes straight for the mail as soon as he comes in.
- *Solution: Hide the mail and give it to him after you kiss. After a few days, he won't even look for the mail anymore.*

By the end of their first month of marriage, Karen was steaming. Apparently her husband, Keith, would walk in at the end of the day and, before even acknowledging her presence, would make a beeline for the mail. "Keith loves catalogs," said Karen, "and we would get at least five a day. Why he couldn't wait a few minutes to look at exercise equipment, outdoor camping gear, or lawn and garden furniture is beyond me."

After taking my *Light His Fire* class, Karen came up with the idea to replace the mail with a note telling Keith where to find her. The note might tell him to look in their bedroom closet, behind a couch, or under a table. Whenever he found Karen, Keith got a ten-second kiss. They've been married nine years, and Keith has learned. The mail can wait!

- Excuse #9: I want to give my wife a ten-second kiss, but she's afraid it will always lead to sex.
- *Solution: Don't let it. Kiss her to show her you love her, rather than as a means to an end.*

Gary was determined to learn to kiss his wife,

Pam, without pushing her to have sex. "I promised myself I would give Pam a ten-second kiss seven days in a row without letting her know I wanted to make love to her," said Gary. "I did it! Or at least I would have done it if, by the fifth day, Pam hadn't dragged *me* into the bedroom."

- Excuse #10: I'd like to give my boyfriend a ten-second kiss, but we only see each other once or twice during the week and usually it's in a public place, like a restaurant. It's too embarrassing to kiss each other like that in public.
- *Solution: I agree. Why not meet in the parking lot instead and give each other the kiss there?*

Ken and Gail had been dating for about six months and usually met for dinner once or twice a week. Gail complained that because they met at a restaurant, they initially felt awkward with each other. They would just greet each other with a peck on the cheek and then would start talking about their day at work. "It felt like we were stuck. I wanted more intimacy, but didn't know how to create it," she said.

Gail started listening to the *Light His Fire* tapes and realized she could cause some real changes to occur in her relationship with Ken. She told him that the next time they had plans for dinner, she wanted to meet in the parking lot of the restaurant instead of inside. He agreed.

To Ken's surprise, when Gail arrived she motioned him into her car. Then she asked him if she could try a little experiment. Intrigued, Ken asked what kind of experiment. "I just want to give you a ten-second kiss," Gail replied. Ken grinned and said, "Absolutely!" Gail had a little timer with her that counted down the seconds, and when the time was up, Gail asked Ken what he thought. Jokingly Ken replied, "I loved the kiss, but the timer has to go."

The Action Causes the Attraction

Once the excuses listed above were matched up with solutions, the mate in each story had a plan of action. Do you know why so many relationships don't last? It's because the couples forget their plan of action. They forget what they did in the beginning.

- What they did was *kiss*.
- What they did was *make each other feel special*.
- What they did was *talk*.
- What they did was *listen*.
- What they did was *hug*.
- What they did was *spend time alone together*.

They fell in love because of their actions.

Of the many stories that I've collected over the years of teaching *Light Her Fire,* one of my favorites is the following:

In his youth, John saw the most beautiful woman on a bus. "I decided to marry her," he said. "Courtship would be a mere formality. But what to say to begin the courtship? 'Would you like some of my gum?' seemed too low-class. 'Hello' was too trite a greeting for my future bride. 'I love you! I am hot with passion!' was too forward. 'I want

*to make you the mother of my children' seemed a bit prema-
ture.*

*Nothing. That's right, I said nothing. And after a while,
the bus reached her stop, she got off, and I never saw her
again. End of story."*

The moral of the story is—you guessed it—if you
do nothing, nothing will change. For things to change,
you've got to change.

A Dose of Confidence

The first time I was asked to be a guest on a TV
show, which happened to be *Geraldo,* I was scared to
death. I could easily have turned down the opportunity, based on my feelings: I had never done anything
like it before; I was scared—make that terrified; and I
was unprepared.

Of course, I didn't let my fear stop me. I just ac-
knowledged it and went on the show anyway. As a
result, my book *Light His Fire* went on to the *New York
Times* best-seller list. I took the action necessary to
promote the book, and as a result of my doing I completely changed my thoughts and feelings about ap-
pearing on TV. After the show, the first thing I did
was shout a triumphant "Yes!" Then the positive
thoughts and feelings started to flow. "I did it! I can't
believe how well it went. I'm so proud of myself. If I
can do this, I can do anything. Look out talk shows,
here I come!"

Do you see how my actions caused my confidence,
how I did what I feared and the confidence came as a

result? Whatever it is that you want to do, just do it. Have the experience, perform the deed, take the plunge—and then evaluate it. Just imagine how different your life could be if you started living by this rule. Don't be like so many people who spend all of their time and energy afraid of life instead of jumping into the middle of it.

A Lesson in Courage

Take a lesson from John, a man in his early thirties, who confided to me one night after class that he wanted to learn to do country-and-western line dancing. I asked him why he didn't just do it, and he replied by giving me a list of reasons as long as my arm:

- I have two left feet.
- I don't have anyone to dance with.
- I might make a fool of myself.
- I'm afraid everybody will stare at me.
- I know people will laugh at me.
- I won't be able to keep up with everybody else.

He could have kept going, but I stopped him. "That's enough thinking and feeling," I said firmly. "Now, here's what you're going to do."

- Call your adult-education program and see when the next class begins.
- Sign up for lessons and pay your money.
- Take the lesson.
- Buy yourself some cowboy boots and a hat.

- Go to the country-and-western dance club nearest you.
- Get in line and dance!

Most people who see me on a talk show or watch John line dance will think we were always sure of ourselves. Of course that isn't true. We had to take the plunge in spite of our fear, and then we had to practice to become good at what we were doing. The first time you try the ten-second kiss with your mate, you may lack confidence. You may even feel nervous and self-conscious. The kiss itself may feel a bit contrived. So what! Practice makes perfect. What's more, you'll have fun in the process of practicing.

What's That in Your Mouth?

Over the years, I've had several dentists in my class, and they've taught me a lot about lips, mouths, and tongues. For example, did you know that there are more nerve endings per square inch on our lips and tongue than anywhere else in our bodies? No wonder we enjoy kissing so much.

Our mouths and lips are sensitive to the smallest amount of pressure. Haven't we all experienced what it feels like to have a hair in our mouth? Until you get rid of it, it drives you wild. If there was a hair on your bed, you certainly wouldn't roll over to escape its pressure on your back. And what about that husk of popcorn wedged between your teeth? It feels like a boulder and you'll do anything to get it out, even pry it out with a matchbook cover. The tongue is so sensitive that different areas of it are specific to only one particular taste. Saltiness, sweetness, sourness, and bitterness are each tasted by a different part of the tongue.

When you and your mate kiss for ten seconds, use this sensitivity to explore all the nuances of a kiss. Try less pressure, more pressure, touch with your tongue here, then there, then somewhere else. Kissing has often been called an art. Who knows, with practice maybe you'll become another Picasso.

As you kiss be aware of the sound and feel of each other's breath, as well. Although we may think we're holding our breath while kissing, we are actually exchanging our breath with each other. That's the reason why kissing is even more intimate than intercourse. When we exchange breath, we are breathing in our mate's life force, his energy, and he is breathing in ours. In this way, we actually become one.

First Kiss

I've never met anyone who didn't remember their first kiss. I certainly remember my first one thirty-seven years ago.

My parents were very strict and I was not allowed to date until I was sixteen. The boys I went out with were just friends. When I met Steve in my junior year I had never been kissed. On our first date, we went to the high school dance. We agreed that we should dance with other people but would save the last dance for each other. We wound up dancing the last two slow dances together.

We talked the entire time on the bus ride home. It felt so natural to ask him to come in and finish our conversation. We sat in the living room and talked for another two hours. I remember having a piece of hard candy in my mouth when out of the blue Steve asked, "When are you going to finish that candy?" The question took me by surprise and I asked, "Why do you want to know?"

"Because I want to kiss you."

My heart started pounding as I realized that I was going to get my first real kiss. How could he want to kiss me with braces on my teeth? What if his lip got caught on the metal? Obviously, he didn't care. He was focused on only one thing.

I kept the candy in my mouth as long as I could, but the moment had finally come. He put his arms around me, pulled me close and gave me THE KISS. The fireworks began and I never wanted the night to end. When people ask me if it was love at first sight, I always say, "No, it was love at first kiss."

Steve gave me my first kiss, but it was not to be my last. In the next few years, I dated and kissed many young men, but nothing ever came close to the feeling I had with Steve. Six years later, I married the man who gave me my first kiss.

I love Stephanie's story of how she was initiated into the world of kissing. Technically, Stephanie's first kiss wasn't a real kiss. But in her mind, it was.

She was fifteen and had never gone to a coed party before. "When I walked into the party, I heard loud music and saw groups of boys and girls talking with each other," said Stephanie. "My first thought was, 'I want to go home.' Then I saw everyone lining up boy-girl-boy-girl in two separate lines. Before I knew it, my girlfriend had grabbed me and stuck me in a line behind a really cute boy who played trumpet in our high school marching band."

Without knowing it, Stephanie was in line for a relay race called Pass the Life Saver. In this game, the person at the front of the line has to pass a Life Saver on a toothpick to the person behind him or her, using only their lips or teeth to hold the toothpick. The goal was to pass it without touching each other's lips. If lips touched, it was just a hazard of the game, of course.

"I'll never forget standing on tiptoe, holding onto this cute boy's shoulders, while he tried to pass the Life Saver to me on a toothpick," said Stephanie. "For one wonderful moment, our lips touched as we worked to pass the toothpick from his mouth to mine. As brief as it was, that was my first kiss, and I will never forget it."

Chip, a man in my *Light Her Fire* class, told us the story of his first kiss. He was just twelve years old and he was at the county fair with his buddies. They spent all day riding the roller coaster, eating corn dogs, and practicing their aim at the shooting gallery.

"I remember every time we'd walk from the shooting gallery to the roller coaster, we'd pass a kissing booth. My buddies acted grossed out when they saw it. I pretended to be repulsed as well, but secretly, I wanted to get kissed." Chip got his chance when all his friends decided to go through the haunted house. He told them he had to use the bathroom. Instead he ran to the kissing booth.

"I knew I was risking getting caught by my

friends, but I didn't care. I had to have a kiss," said Chip. "I got in line and when it was my turn to be kissed, my ears started ringing and I thought I was going to faint. Right when I was going to pass out, I felt a pair of warm, moist lips cover my entire mouth. Man, that was the best thing I had ever felt! To this day, no one from that group of friends knows what I did."

Margaret still blushes when she tells the story of her first kiss. "Because I was almost twenty years old and had waited so long to date, my first kiss felt larger than life," she says. "All my friends had already been kissed lots of times, so I had heard many versions of what a first kiss could be like." The night of Margaret's first kiss, she was at a cast party after performing in a community theater production. "Throughout the run of the show, I had a big crush on Jason, who played the lead. Since I was in the chorus, we didn't get to know each other very well, but he had always been friendly to me."

At the end of the party, Jason asked Margaret if she wanted to get a bite to eat. Margaret agreed, and they went to an all-night diner. "After we ate, Jason drove me back to my car, which was parked in front of the house where the party had been. We talked some more in the car and then I finally said, 'Well, I guess I better go.'

"I remember reaching for the car door handle, but my hand wouldn't pull the latch to open the door. I wanted so much for Jason to kiss me. One, two, three seconds went by. 'Come on,' I thought. 'Kiss me!'

"Then I felt Jason's right hand behind my head pulling me toward his face. I felt his warm breath on my mouth as he opened his mouth to kiss me. I remember closing my eyes and feeling totally engulfed by him as our lips separated and met again several times, each time with more passion.

"When it was time to get out of the car, Jason had to put on the defroster because we had fogged up the windows so much. The windows may have been foggy, but I knew then and there that the memory of my first kiss would remain crystal clear in my mind forever."

You've Lost That Loving Feeling

Chances are, somewhere in your relationship, you and your mate kissed like this. So what happened? Why did it change from a long, passionate, open-mouthed kiss to a quick peck on the lips or cheek? The answer is that in the beginning of your relationship you saw each other as lovers, but as the years passed, you became so involved in your chores, duties, and all your other responsibilities that you forgot to take time for each other. You forgot how to be lovers.

Think back to the way you greeted each other in the beginning of your relationship. I'm sure you stopped whatever you were doing, smiled, embraced, and kissed. Even though you may have had family pressures, money problems, job issues, and a whole host of other difficulties, you still managed to focus on your mate and the kiss.

Compare that earlier greeting when you both felt special, needed, and desirable, to the way you greet your mate today. Are you on the phone or at the computer? Are you working in the kitchen or involved with the children? Are you in the backyard talking to a neighbor? When chores and duties are more important than greeting our mates, we send a message that says, "You are no longer a priority in my life."

We all want to feel special. Why do you think we always announce our arrival? What man or woman doesn't say, "Hi, I'm home" or ask, "Anybody home?" We do it because we want to be recognized. When there's only a verbal response like, "I'm in the den" or "I'm on the phone," with no physical connection, feelings of emptiness and isolation occur. Many men and women have told me that even though they look forward all day to being with their mate, for some unknown reason they feel lonely as soon as they're with their mate again.

Since it's impossible to feel isolated and connected at the same time, the solution is simple. The solution is the ten-second kiss.

A Reason to Kiss

You don't have to limit your kiss to a greeting. Since the purpose of the kiss is to promote closeness, warmth, and passion, you can do it anywhere, anytime, for any reason. Why not have some fun and come up with places and reasons to kiss? Here are a few suggestions:

- Roadside Kissing. Stand near a busy road and both of you select a car color—Let's say it's red. Every time you see a red car kiss for ten seconds.

- Movie Kissing. The next time you go to a movie and the actors begin kissing, give each other a ten-second kiss.
- Party Kissing. Just before you leave for the party, decide in advance what your private signal to each other will be. Whenever you wish, catch your mate's eye and give the appropriate signal. While everyone else is engaged in conversation, you'll be engaged in a ten-second kiss.
- Sport Kissing. Every time your favorite team scores a point, it's time to score with your mate. If your baseball team scores a run, your football team scores a touchdown, or your hockey team scores a goal, you score a ten-second kiss.
- Sitcom Kissing. Select a word or someone's name and every time one of the characters on your favorite TV show repeats what you've chosen, it's time to kiss for ten seconds.

I'm sure you can think of other opportunities to connect with your mate. There are probably many times when you have shared an experience together and yet, when you arrive home, you don't feel any closer. Or you've spent the evening watching TV together and you go to bed feeling distant. It's because there was no physical connection. You have the power to change that.

The K.I.S.S. Plan

What follows is an action plan to help you bring back the passion and love in your relationship. I assure you that it does not matter that you got this idea from a book. What matters is that you want to feel close and connected again. Using the K.I.S.S. Plan is a way of overriding any feelings of loneliness or separateness you may be experiencing in your relationship and taking action to **Keep It Something Special**.

The plan is simple. I want you to shock your mate this week with a wonderful, passionate ten-second kiss. You may choose to do this in the morning or in the evening, but I want it to be a surprise. I don't want the two of you to have a conversation about whether or not you should do this. The only way you're going to see the result is to just do it!

After your mate says, "Wow, what in the world has gotten into you?" you can then explain the ten-second kiss. Tell your mate that whenever you haven't seen each other for any significant length of time, you are going to wrap your arms around each other and kiss for at least ten seconds. Let your mate know that it doesn't matter what kind of day either of you has had, you're going to kiss for a minimum of ten seconds, no matter what!

Set a timer in the beginning. Ten seconds doesn't sound like a long time, but you'll probably be surprised at how long it seems when you're engaged in an intimate kiss. Whether you kiss in the morning before you go your separate ways, or you greet each other with a kiss at the end of the day, you'll feel closer and more connected than you have in a long time. You may enjoy it so much that you'll decide to kiss passionately twice a day, and what started out as an obligatory exercise will soon become a much welcomed lifestyle change.

By the way, the longest kiss recorded in *The Guinness Book of World Records* is 417 hours. Just be glad I'm only asking you for ten seconds!

2

THE FIVE-SECOND COMPLIMENT

*A*side from being a wonderful habit to acquire, your ten-second kiss is a daily reminder to keep your relationship something special. To do that, you must treat it as if it were your most treasured possession.

Pretend for a moment that you've inherited a priceless family heirloom that has been passed down to you from preceding generations. It is chock-full of genealogical history and meaning. Wouldn't you be sure to keep it safe from harm, either by storing it in a secure place or displaying it in a protected area in your home?

Well, your relationship with your mate is much more precious than any heirloom. A relationship is more than just two people living side by side. It is a refuge against the world, a place to feel safe, to be nurtured, to grow. In a relationship, each individual has the perfect opportunity to become more than they could ever be alone. Your relationship is much more than the sum total of its parts. As a unit, the two of you are a much stronger force than you are as individuals.

Laurie, a woman in one of my classes, learned the hard way just how valuable her marriage was.

It was a sweltering summer day in her neighborhood. Laurie's two kids were playing with their friends on the front lawn; her husband, Jim, was in the bedroom changing out of his work clothes; and she was cooking dinner.

Suddenly Laurie heard a loud banging on her side door. She opened it to find her next-door neighbor's teenage daughter trying to remain calm as she said, "Don't panic, but your house is on fire. My mom has already called 9-1-1."

"From that moment on, everything seemed to move in slow motion," Laurie says. "I remember running to the front door and screaming for the kids to stay outside. Then, realizing Jim was in our bedroom, I raced up the stairs yelling for him to get out of the house."

What baffled Laurie was that she didn't smell smoke or hear any smoke alarms. It wasn't until she tried to go up the stairs to the third floor that she figured out why. The fire had started in the attic, so all the smoke and flames were going out the third-floor windows.

Laurie and her husband grabbed their two cats, her purse, and the car phone, gathered the children, and ran across the street to a neighbor's front lawn.

There the family stood huddled together weeping as they watched everything they had worked for and cherished go up in smoke.

During the three hours it took the firemen to put out the blaze, Laurie did a mental inventory of each floor. As she watched the firemen break every second-floor window, Laurie thought about all that was being destroyed—her children's toys, memorabilia collected over the years, family photo albums.

After the fire was out, the firemen let Laurie and her husband back into their home. Stepping over the charred rubble, the firemen led them from room to room to assess the damage. Finding their way to their bedroom, Laurie shone a flashlight around the room. Between the fire and the water and smoke damage, there was little left of what was once their love nest. As the flashlight illuminated the corner where the remains of her nightstand stood, Laurie got a shock! Amazingly, the only thing in the room that did not have water or ashes on it was a book on the bedside table Laurie had just begun to read. It was *Expect a Miracle.*

Laurie turned to her husband and held him in her arms. It had just sunk in that what she was looking at was the fire-blackened remains of the very spot where either of them might have been sleeping when the fire started. It was a miracle that they were all safe. Yes, they had lost irreplaceable photos, gifts their kids had made for them since preschool, and a valuable collection of Japanese china that Laurie had inherited from her mother—but they still had each other!

Since the fire, Laurie and Jim treasure their relationship in a way they never did before, and to keep it something special they begin and end each day with a ten-second kiss.

Knowledge Is Power

What you are about to read is the most valuable information you'll ever receive regarding your love life. It is so valuable that you should read it several times, underline it, say it out loud, write it down on a separate note card, and share it with everyone!

We fall in love with a man or a woman because of *the way we feel about ourselves* when we are with them.

Women take note:
- A man will fall in love with you and *stay* in love with you because of the way he feels about *himself* when he is with you.

Men heed this:
- A woman will fall in love with you and *stay* in love with you because of the way she feels about *herself* when she is with you.

Trust me: no one has ever told me they fell in love with their mate because they were insulting, condescending, or sarcastic. All the men I've interviewed agree that when they fell in love, they felt stronger, sexier, more capable, more intelligent, and more important than they had felt before this special woman came into their life. The women I interview tell me that they felt prettier, sexier, more intelligent, and more capable when they finally met "Mr. Right" than they had ever felt about themselves before.

So to attract and keep a mate who is hopelessly and passionately in love with you, you must help your partner feel good about himself or herself.

You will not learn how to make more money, become more attractive, or lose weight in this book. Do you know why? Because some of the most attractive people in the world don't have a love relationship. Some of the wealthiest people are lonely. Some of the slimmest are without a partner. You are going to learn that really loving someone means making them feel better about themselves than anyone else can.

I receive letters like this one all of the time, reinforcing this simple concept:

Dear Ellen,

For the past five years I've been dating with disastrous results. I have a wonderful job, earn a comfortable living, and have been told that I am attractive and intelligent. So why then did I not get a second date or even a phone call from the guys I went out with? I just figured they were all jerks!

I attended one of your seminars and realized that I was always worried about making a good impression. I worried about looking good, smelling good, and sounding good. I never thought about making my date feel good. Well, you gave me a whack on the head with a 2 x 4. I want you to know that I'm now dating the greatest guy. We're talking about getting married and it's all because of what you said. I stopped worrying about the impression I was making and began focusing on how terrific he was.

Thanks for making me see that I needed to change the direction of my focus.

Here is a letter I received from a woman who had been married for fifteen years. In it she tells what happened when she stopped being the enemy and began to show her husband some appreciation:

For the past few years I've been unhappy and have experienced a vague feeling of dissatisfaction with day-to-day living.

It struck me that if only I could see things in a different light, I might be happier, but I was at a loss about how to make that happen. I was always mad at my husband, snapping at the kids, and frustrated with my futile attempts to change the situation.

Since taking your workshop, I've discovered that I can change the way I feel by changing the way I act. As a result, our entire family life has improved dramatically. Recently my husband was on a business trip for eight days. I don't like it when he's gone and usually I'm nasty for days before his departure. By the time he leaves, we are both so angry with each other that I wonder why he comes back.

This time, not only did I avoid being a shrew, I tucked seven greeting cards into his suitcase, one for each day that he was gone. While he was away, he sent me a dozen long-stemmed red roses in a box with a huge bow around it.

The day he was to arrive home, the children and I decorated the house and put up "Welcome Home Daddy" signs. When he came in at two in the morning from a late flight, there were flowers, streamers, balloons and love notes to greet him. And he knew beyond a shadow of a doubt, that he is loved more than words can say, unconditionally, forever.

His Greatest Cheerleader, Her Greatest Fan

One of the keys to keeping your relationship special is understanding that you and your mate are on the same team. And whether it is a sports team, a strategic planning team, or a medical team, teammates support each other. If a baseball player steps up to the plate and strikes out, his fellow teammates don't yell, "Aw, you stink! Get back to the dugout and stay there!" They pat him on the back and say, "Hey, tough break, but you'll do it next time." Members of the same team hold a vision for one another. And in case a team player loses sight of his vision, all of his teammates are there to remind him of it.

Tragically, after many years together, lots of couples lose the vision they had at the beginning and see each other only one way—negatively. When this happens, it doesn't take long for them to begin to feel poorly about themselves when they are together.

A man or woman who receives criticism instead of compliments will often let their eyes wander until they lock onto someone new—someone who makes them feel good about themselves. You wouldn't believe how many letters I get telling me essentially the same story as this one, from John. In his letter he explains how he came close to becoming involved in an affair with a woman he had met while innocently standing in line for popcorn at a football game. They struck up a conversation and discovered they worked in the same profession. After swapping business cards, they extended a polite, "Call me if I can ever be of assistance."

Three weeks later his new acquaintance called

him. They had coffee. A month later he found himself
drinking a lot more coffee than he ever had before.

"When I was with this woman, I could do no
wrong," he writes. "She laughed at my jokes. She
asked my advice. After a few conversations with her,
I felt better about myself than I had in the twenty-two
years I'd been with my wife."

John goes on to say that even though he was very
tempted, he loved his wife and valued the years they
had spent together. "Luckily for us, I saw your infomercial and sent for your tapes right away. I had
already told my wife about the other woman, so she
was as motivated as I was to change things. We've
been listening to them and applying the principles
faithfully and the future is looking very good."

Here's the story of a woman whose birthday gift
from her husband was the catalyst that ended their
marriage. "My business had been slow for months
and our income had dropped by about half," Janet
told me. "My husband became preoccupied with the
state of our finances, and for months our conversations and arguments revolved around getting out of
debt. Although our financial situation was grim, my
husband was obsessed with it. We were always fight-
ing about money. In an effort to help me increase my
clientele he gave me a subscription to the Internet for
my birthday."

Alone in her office all day, trying to drum up new
clients, Janet spent a lot of time on-line in "chat
rooms." It was in a "chat room" that she met a single
man with whom she became friendly.

It wasn't long before their conversations turned
from small talk to intimate details about her marital

problems. "Whenever I talked to my Internet friend, I felt listened to, that my ideas and feelings were worthwhile. With my husband, I felt like nothing I said was important. When I met this man on-line, I realized how little I was getting from my husband."

After eight months of on-line intimacy and cyber-sex, Janet realized that she wanted a more fulfilling relationship and decided to leave her husband.

"Now that I've left him, my husband wants to work on our marriage," said Janet. "I guess I should be happy, but it hurts that I had to leave him to get his attention."

Unfortunately, Janet's husband neglected to be her biggest fan. He must have been at one time, or she wouldn't have married him. But instead of cheering her on in her business, he caved in to his fear and made the state of their finances his priority.

The absolute best insurance for keeping your relationship as strong as it can be is simply this: build each other up, rather than tearing each other down. Be teammates, not competitors. Together, you'll not only create a winning team—you'll have more fun playing the game.

Dean loves to share his story of the way his wife supported him during the scariest transition of his life.

After years of hating his job, Dean decided he had to change careers. He had started medical school in his youth, but had had to quit for financial reasons. He'd always regretted it, and now he wanted to finish what he'd started. At forty-three years old, Dean came home from work one day and told his wife that he wanted to become a doctor. Mia smiled and said,

"Great, honey," never dreaming that he'd go through with it.

"With a year and a half left in my schooling, we would be incurring a debt of $150,000 while our contemporaries were planning for retirement. It scared us both. But the hardest part of it all was not being at home much," said Dean. "Last year my daughter's school had a father-daughter event. There was no way I could go, and I felt awful. Med school wasn't easy on Mia either. She's a social worker and does a lot of counseling. At one point, she confessed that she felt like she was being tested on everything she counsels others for. Thank goodness she passed."

There were times when Dean was afraid their marriage wouldn't withstand the demands on it. Fortunately, it did, and he says the main reason is because Mia supported him in his dream to become a doctor. "It was a team effort," he says. "Now it's my turn to support her."

One of the most touching and inspiring stories I've ever heard was from a woman who credits her husband with saving her life.

When Nadine reaches into the toe of her Christmas stocking each year, she finds a G.I. Joe toy soldier. It never fails to remind her of the healing power of her husband's love.

Joel and Nadine were married in 1983. They struggled with infertility problems, and by 1987, Nadine sensed something was really wrong. She requested exploratory surgery and the procedure revealed a tumor on her right ovary. Further testing showed that Nadine had ovarian cancer.

Two weeks later she entered the hospital for the

first of twelve chemotherapy treatments. Joel was by her side from lunchtime through evening. "I know how helpless he felt," said Nadine.

The next morning she woke up in her hospital room to find an army of G.I. Joe action figures lined up on the windowsill, aiming their rifles at a cardboard replica Joel had made of her cancer-ridden ovary. Behind the troop of G.I. Joes was the commander in chief, Super Ovary, a cardboard representation of a healthy ovary wearing tennis shoes and a big "S" on its chest.

Over the next several months, Nadine's windowsill overflowed with G.I. Joes. Nurses from other floors came to visit her just to see her collection and meet the man who had started the war against his wife's cancer.

"It's been ten years since my diagnosis," says Nadine, "and I'm convinced I'm cancer-free because I have a husband who loves me so much that he'll call in the troops."

A Winning Combination

The football teams that make it to the Super Bowl and the baseball teams that make it to the World Series share something in common: they have a good combination of players.

Coaches don't expect all of their players to have the same qualities and strengths. Owners and managers work really hard at picking players with the right combination of skills and talents to make up a winning team. If you were to line up the whole team, each player would have a different set of skills than the player standing next to him. It's the combination of everyone's talents put together that makes a winning team.

You and your mate are a team too. For your relationship to get to the top and stay there, you must recognize and appreciate the different traits you each bring to the playing field.

One man in my *Light Her Fire* class was at the end of his rope with his wife. "I feel like I'm married to a fish," he'd say. "I'm forever reeling her in."

Week after week this man would come to the class and tell stories about how disorganized his wife was. One week she'd run out of gas, another week she'd lost her credit card, and yet another, she'd locked her keys in the car.

One night he told the class this story. "My mother-in-law was donating a huge sum of money to a charity and had requested that my wife and I deliver it for her," he began. "She gave my wife the check, but the night before our appointment my wife couldn't find it. We spent hours tearing apart the house, turning her purse and pockets inside out, and searching the car. Finally my wife said, 'I wonder if I could have thrown it out with the garbage?'

" 'How could you have done that?' I bellowed.

" 'Well,' she said, 'I was paying bills, and I had this huge pile of paper to throw away, and I just scooped them into the wastebasket. I think the check was in that pile.' "

After what seemed like an hour spent sifting through the garbage, he found it. "It was soggy and smelly and I told my wife I would not go with her to deliver a $1,000 check that had coffee stains on it."

Instead of commiserating, the class roared.

By the end of the six-week class, this man had learned to see his wife as he had in the beginning of their relationship. He remembered that her carefree nature had charmed him and he understood that it balanced his tendency to be overly fretful. Sure, she was disorganized, but she was also a lot of fun. He realized that together they made a pretty good team. Fishing didn't turn out to be so bad after all.

One woman in the *Light His Fire* workshop told the class that she would frequently look at her husband and ask, "Is anybody in there?" She admitted to being on the emotional side, and she couldn't understand how her husband remained so calm and unemotional. "Flat" was how she described him.

She recalled the time their six-month-old son was to have neurosurgery. "There we were at the door to the operating room, handing over our precious baby to the surgeon. I was an emotional wreck—crying, shaking, nauseous with fear. I looked at my husband and he was as unruffled as could be. I couldn't believe it. How could he be so calm? I remember asking him if he had ice water running through his veins."

After understanding the way two people work together as a team, this woman actually thanked her husband for the qualities he displayed the day of their son's operation. While she was a basket case, his calm manner allowed him to listen carefully to what the doctor said, ask questions about their child's condition, and be the strong, grounded teammate that she needed at the time. When she looked back on the ordeal, she realized that it was the combination of their different personalities that got them through their son's diagnosis, surgery, and recovery.

Make My Day

How long do you think it might take to make your mate feel good, to make his or her day? Five seconds. That's right! Only five seconds to turn a frown into a smile and put a bounce in his or her step for the rest of the day. It will make your mate's day to know that:

- You feel you are the luckiest person alive to have him or her in your life.
- You can't imagine what your life would be like without him or her.
- Your mate is the best thing that ever happened to you.
- Your mate makes you very happy.

But for your mate to know you feel these things, they have to be verbalized. You have to *say* them! "Oh, oh," I can almost hear you thinking. "Here comes the hard part. I've never been good at expressing my feelings."

Well, I think you'll agree that even the most shy, reserved, or withdrawn person can manage to give a five-second compliment. Even the busiest, most preoccupied, or self-absorbed person can take five seconds out of their day to make their mate feel special. Once you start giving your mate a five-second compliment, it will quickly become a habit, you'll become really good at it, and you'll find you enjoy the results.

Many of us have a difficult time accepting compliments. We were taught that we are conceited if we feel good about ourselves or acknowledge our good qualities. If your mate squirms with embarrassment when complimented, start out small. For instance you could say something like, "You make the best coffee I've ever tasted," or "The lawn looks great. All your hard work paid off." Eventually your mate will begin to feel comfortable enough to accept a more personal compliment, such as, "You look so beautiful tonight," or "You have such a muscular build." If they object by saying something like, "Oh, stop it. You're embarrassing me," you can respond with, "So divorce me and tell the judge I compliment you too much!"

If you have a hard time receiving a compliment, try to remember that giving and receiving are the same thing. When you can accept a compliment graciously you are actually giving your mate a gift.

It feels so much better to give a compliment to someone who can accept it graciously than to give one to someone who says, "Oh, thanks, but I think I look fat in this dress," or "Thanks, but my hair looks better short," or "Thanks, but I cooked the roast too long."

Dick admired his wife's figure very much. As the years passed he was always impressed by how slim and trim Diane remained. Whenever he saw her step out of the shower he would say, "You know, you have the figure of a twenty-two-year-old."

Instead of accepting the compliment, Diane would say something like, "No, I don't. Look at my thighs. I have huge saddlebags. My waist is thickening. I have no hips or breasts. I look like a boy." Eventually Dick stopped telling her how good she looked. Diane missed his compliments and couldn't understand why he had stopped, until she took my class and realized she was shooting down everything wonderful he said about her.

Accepting a compliment from your mate is a way of loving them by letting them love you. The best way I can think of to explain it is like this. Suppose your five-year-old son came home from kindergarten and proudly presented you with a valentine he had made in class. You wouldn't dream of treating it in an offhand way: "Oh, thanks, but I really don't deserve this." You'd open your heart and your arms to that little boy and you'd let him know how much his love meant to you. That's how we should accept a compliment from our mate—with an open heart. When Dick told Diane how good she looked, it wasn't about a bathing-beauty competition. It was about love.

Some of you reading this may think your mate has no qualities worth complimenting. Well, I challenge you on that. When you met him or her, you could have made a list of qualities as long as your arm saying what you loved about your partner. But somehow, over time, those qualities you loved have become qualities that annoy you. I'm here to tell you that those qualities you once loved in your mate are still there. It's your perception that has changed.

You can see any one of your mate's qualities in either a positive light or a negative light. The choice is yours. Ask yourself this question: "If I continue to concentrate on what my mate is lacking, what my mate hasn't accomplished, what my mate is always doing wrong, and how my mate doesn't ever measure up to my expectations, what will my payoff be?'' In case you don't know the answer, I'll tell you. Your payoff will be a cold, unresponsive, angry person.

If, on the other hand, you choose to concentrate on your mate's strengths, if you notice all the little things your mate does for you, if you praise your mate for their small accomplishments, reinforce your mate's capabilities, and appreciate your mate's value as a human being, your payoff will be a warm, loving, passionate, and devoted partner.

Let's compare the personality traits that you now may see as bad, negative, or wrong to the way you saw these same traits when you first fell in love. Then I will show you what to say to turn a complaint into a thoughtful, loving, five-second compliment.

- **What you saw** (in the beginning): She's so outgoing, always the life of the party.
- **What you see** (after a couple of years): She never stops talking. She draws so much attention to herself it's embarrassing.
- **What you say** (to make your mate feel special): *You're such a good conversationalist. There are never any awkward silences with you around.*

- **What you saw** (in the beginning): He's so knowledgeable. He's like a walking encyclopedia.
- **What you see** (after a couple of years): He thinks he's an expert on everything.
- **What you say** (to make your mate feel special):

You are so smart. You retain so much information. There doesn't seem to be anything you don't know.

- **What you saw** (in the beginning): She is so efficient and organized.
- **What you see** (after a couple of years): She is too structured.
- **What you say** (to make your mate feel special): *Everything is always in its place. I never have a problem finding anything when I need it.*

- **What you saw** (in the beginning): He has goals and dreams.
- **What you see** (after a couple of years): He is a workaholic.
- **What you say** (to make your mate feel special): *You are amazing. You know where you want to go and what you want to accomplish, and you do whatever is necessary to make that happen.*

- **What you saw** (in the beginning): She is so economical.
- **What you see** (after a couple of years): She is stingy.
- **What you say** (to make your mate feel special): *You work hard at saving money for our future. That gives me a secure feeling.*

- **What you saw** (in the beginning): He is even-tempered and easygoing.
- **What you see** (after a couple of years): He is void of emotion.
- **What you say** (to make your mate feel special):

You are so calm and serene, such a stable force in our family.

- **What you saw** (in the beginning): She has a lot of energy.
- What you see (after a couple of years): She never sits still.
- **What you say** (to make your mate feel special): *You can get more done in an hour than I can in a day.*

- **What you saw** (in the beginning): He is so affectionate.
- **What you see** (after a couple of years): He is oversexed.
- **What you say** (to make your mate feel special): *You are so demonstrative with your love, always willing to hold hands, rub my back, or cuddle.*

Affair-Proof Your Relationship

When you see your mate's qualities as only negative, you risk the chance that someone else will see those same qualities as positive. If your mate rarely gets a compliment from you, he or she won't feel good in your presence. Eventually your mate may meet someone who sees the good in him or her and verbalizes it. Your mate will like how this feels, and before you know it, the stage is set for an affair.

I remember one night after class one of my students stayed to speak with me. She was distraught because her fiancé had broken their engagement. When I asked her what had happened, she explained that during their courtship, he'd worked in the corporate world, but six months before their wedding date, he decided to quit the corporate world and go back to school to get his teaching credential.

Ann tried everything she could to convince him not to leave the business world. She ended up telling him she thought he was crazy, that he would never make enough money teaching. He went back to school in spite of Ann's protests, and in one of his classes he met a woman who was studying for the same degree he was. This woman told him she admired him for quitting the business rat race. She pumped him up and gave him daily encouragement. A month before he was supposed to marry Ann, he called off the engagement. He had fallen in love with his classmate.

Would this story have turned out differently if Ann had been on her fiancé's team? Absolutely. If she had verbalized her faith in him and complimented him on his courage and perseverance, he wouldn't have needed someone else to make him feel good.

A letter from Judy recounted how a lack of attention and compliments from her husband almost led to the end of their marriage.

My husband was depressed because he was unhappy in his job. To make up for a dull career, he spent many evenings attending school board and city council meetings. I was definitely neglected.

I met this younger man through a friend of my daughter's. He was a college student and needed a place to stay over the summer. I offered an extra bedroom in our home. While living with us, he spent a lot of time watching me

cook, decorate, and garden. He couldn't say enough won-
derful things about my domesticity. That whole summer,
all I heard was, "You have such a green thumb", or "You
have a flair for color and texture", or "You make better
spaghetti sauce than my mother". He also made it clear
that he was attracted to me.

Hearing these wonderful things made me realize how
much I was missing in my marriage. When I heard about
your tapes, I decided to send for them and see if there was
anything on them that would help my situation. Fortu-
nately, there was. I began treating my husband with more
love and affection, complimenting him every chance I had,
giving him a ten-second kiss every day. Within a short
time, my husband began to respond in kind. Thank you for
saving my marriage.

Styles of Loving

Pay attention to your mate's actions and you'll see
that every day he or she is showing you in many
ways how much you're loved. Although it may be a
different way than yours, it has just as much value.

Marianne spent much of her adult life feeling sorry
for herself because she didn't think her mother really
loved her. When Marianne was a child, her mother
worked full-time to supplement her husband's income. Because she had grown up in poverty, she
wanted to shower Marianne with all the extras she
had missed in her own childhood. With the extra income she earned, she bought Marianne everything
she ever asked for. To this day, Marianne's basement
is filled with toys from her childhood: a dollhouse,

puppets, a marionette stage, dolls of every kind and description—whatever the latest and greatest "must have" toy of the month was. When Marianne got married, her mother quit working. Marianne was delighted and looked forward to spending the time with her mother that she had missed as a child. However, whenever she would suggest getting together, her mother would have a reason to say, "Not today, honey," or "Maybe another time."

So on Christmas and her birthday, when her mother would shower her with clothes, jewelry, and household items, Marianne would think, "She's just giving me all of this to make up for the time she never spent with me. If she really loved me, she'd say 'yes' when I ask her to get together."

It wasn't until two years before her mother died that Marianne realized that giving her material gifts was her mother's way of loving her.

"Thank God I figured it out. The last two years with my mother were the best ones in our relationship. I finally accepted her gifts and the love that accompanied them, rather than believing my mother didn't love me because she wasn't loving me the way I wanted her to. Miraculously, my mother and I spent more time together those last two years than in the thirty-six years before that."

Betty had been married to Chuck, a construction worker, for twenty-six years, and she feared her marriage was in trouble. Now that the kids were grown and out of the house, she and Chuck had more privacy than they had ever had before, and yet he never approached her. Betty felt that Chuck no longer loved her.

I asked Betty if maybe Chuck was showing his love in another way. "I don't think so," she replied. "He keeps so busy puttering around the house on weekends that he doesn't give me any attention."

Zeroing in on her comment that he was busy puttering, I asked Betty if she could think of anything about Chuck that she admired. She thought long and hard and finally said that he did beautiful work around the house. He had built her a new patio and constructed a little pond with a waterfall in the backyard. He had built her new bookcases in the living room and installed all new carpeting throughout the house.

I explained to Betty that this was Chuck's way of saying "I love you." Here was a man who worked hard all week long in construction and, instead of relaxing on the weekends and taking a break from what he normally did during the week, he spent almost every Saturday and Sunday trying to please her with his handiwork.

I asked her if he knew that she appreciated his efforts. "Well, if you mean do I tell him I do, then the answer is 'no.' I figured he would just know that, after all these years."

I told Betty the reason Chuck wasn't making love to her was that he never felt appreciated. He loved her in his way, not hers. I explained that very few men who worked as hard as he did during the week would have been willing to spend the time doing those projects week after week. I suggested that she start complimenting him and appreciating all that he does or it would only be a matter of time before another woman did. Betty followed my instructions to the letter. Little by little Chuck started feeling better about himself, and guess what? Of all the rooms in the house that Chuck enjoys working in, the bedroom is his favorite!

As you can see, there are many styles of loving, and they are all of value. Although you may prefer a different style, it's important to appreciate the love you get from your mate no matter what form it takes. After all, love is love. It doesn't matter how it's packaged; it's what's inside that counts. We can show love by spending time with our mate, by doing for them, by touching, by being thoughtful.

Look at the examples below and identify which styles of loving are yours and which are your mate's.

Time Spent Together
- Taking a walk with you
- Taking you to a ball game or the theater
- Going away with you for the weekend
- Going shopping with you
- Taking you to dinner
- Going for a drive with you
- Taking you dancing
- Going bike riding with you
- Taking you to a movie
- Going away with you for a vacation
- Relaxing with you in bed on a weekend morning

Service
- Cooking dinner for you
- Picking up your dry cleaning
- Running a hot bubble bath for you

- Fixing things around the house
- Cleaning the garage
- Washing your car
- Doing the laundry
- Mowing the lawn
- Going grocery shopping
- Taking out the trash

Touch

- Holding your hand
- Massaging your neck and shoulders
- Snuggling up to you in bed
- Hugging and kissing you
- Giving you a foot rub
- Scratching your back
- Stroking your hair
- Caressing your face
- Holding you close when dancing

Thoughtfulness

- Calling you in the middle of the day to see how you're doing
- E-mailing you a message to let you know you're being thought of
- Keeping the children quiet so you can sleep an extra hour
- Planning a birthday party for you
- Warming up the car for you
- Leaving the lights on for you if you're coming home late

- Putting on the electric blanket before you come to bed
- Sending you an "I'm thinking of you" card
- Picking up your favorite carry-out meal
- Renting your favorite movie video

We all fall into our own natural way of loving. You and your mate may love each other in one particular style or a combination of styles. Your job is to appreciate and compliment your mate for his or her style of loving you.

The K.I.S.S. Plan

Your relationship is the most precious gift you have. It deserves to be treasured and protected in every way possible. **K**eep **I**t **S**omething **S**pecial with a five-second compliment, and watch your team spirit build.

From now on I want you to look at your mate in a way you never have before. Pay attention to his or her every move with an eye for the positive.

Does she remember to put the cap back on the toothpaste tube? Does he remember to put the toilet seat down? Is she especially patient with the children? Has he overseen a home-repair project particularly well? Make a game of seeing how many wonderful things about him or her you can find that you've been taking for granted.

Remember, you have to verbalize the positive things you notice. Give your partner a compliment at least once a day. Compliment your mate on what he or she stands for, does, and says. Don't forget physical appearance. Before you close your eyes each night, ask yourself, "Have I complimented my mate today?" If you haven't, you owe two for the next day!

At least once a week compliment your partner in front of your children. You are a role model for them. If you brag about their mommy or daddy, they'll store it in their memory bank and do the same with their mate someday.

Once a week compliment your mate in front of other people. When you praise a person in front of others, the compliment has double the impact than when done privately. Your mate may feel embarrassed, but do it anyway. He or she is loving it on the inside.

Get out your pom-poms. Grab your megaphone. Cheer, hoot, holler, and root for your mate! Be your mate's biggest fan and you'll both be winners.

3

THE THIRTY-MINUTE TALK

Slow Down, Please

Susan and Phil, a couple I met at one of my lectures, told me a story that I've retold hundreds of times. They described themselves as being a very active couple. They were involved in a lot of sports, and spent much of their time watching each other participate in either softball games or marathons. Susan watched Phil's softball games several times a week, and Phil cheered from the sidelines whenever Sue ran a marathon.

"We were always so busy with our sports activities that we never took time to just talk to each other," said Susan. "When Phil started playing softball, he began a ritual of going to a sports bar with some of his teammates after the game. I resented it, but I never told him. I wanted him to come home with me after the games, but I wanted him to reach that decision on his own. He never did."

One evening, when Phil was getting ready for a game, he reminded Susan that he'd be going out afterward with the guys. Susan went into a rage.

"I've never seen her that mad," said Phil. "I couldn't understand why she was so angry. I always went out after my games."

As the argument intensified, Susan became so upset she ran out of the house and down the street. Phil instinctively followed her. Susan was a good runner and it took a while for Phil to catch up to her. "By the time I reached her, I was really winded," said Phil. "I pleaded with her to slow down and talk to me. I was so out of breath, I couldn't talk. All I could do was listen. We ended up walking and talking for thirty minutes."

"That was the first time we'd had a heart-to-heart talk in more than a year and a half," said Susan. "It was wonderful."

Susan and Phil told me how that evening changed the nature of their whole marriage. By walking alone together, without the distraction of television, the dog, or the phone, they were able to concentrate on what the other was saying. They have since incorporated a thirty-minute "walking talk" into their daily routine. "On bad-weather days, we turn off the TV, turn down the ringer on the phone, and talk indoors for thirty minutes," said Susan. "We're spoiled now. We want our thirty minutes a day. It's our relationship vitamin!"

An Underwater Adventure

Susan and Phil have committed to keep their relationship something special in a way that I think most couples would envy. A relationship is only as deep as its level of communication. Unless you can share your deepest fears, pain, hopes, and dreams as a couple, your communication will remain on the surface. I believe that if you were to take a survey, most people would say that they would love to communicate more deeply with their mates. The willingness is there. But who's got the time? Who knows how?

You *make* the time. And I'll *teach* you how.

There are many levels at which we can communicate with each other. To make it easier for you to understand the levels of communication that I am talking about, I'm going to compare it to deep-sea diving. Let's imagine that you and your mate are wearing snorkeling gear and are swimming on the surface of the water. Translated into everyday life, this means you are doing things like laundry, washing the car, grocery shopping, car pooling, paying bills, and all the other activities you do in order to exist in your world as a couple. When you communicate about these things, you are communicating at what I call the surface level. At this level, you simply exchange information. You say things like:

- Are you picking the kids up from soccer practice?
- I paid the MasterCard bill today.
- I went to the dentist and had to have a crown put on.

- We're having salmon for dinner tonight.
- I'll be home late because I have a lot of work to do.

Most couples whose communication exists solely at the surface level spend more time watching television than they do connecting with each other. I remember reading a report a few years ago stating that the average American family has the TV on almost seven hours a day, or nearly forty-nine hours a week. The same report said that the average American couple talks only about twenty minutes a week. That's approximately three minutes a day! And when they do talk, this is what they say: "Good morning," "Good night," "I'm home," "What's for dinner," and "Any mail?"

Can you think of any area of your life that would thrive on three minutes of attention a day? If you were taking a class, how good would your grades be if you were studying for only three minutes a day? What would you think of someone's parenting skills if they were spending only three minutes a day with their children? Would it be possible to fall in love and decide to commit to each other if you spent only twenty minutes a week together? So what makes us think that once we are in a long-term relationship, we can spend just three minutes a day connecting with our mate and have a passionate, meaningful relationship? We can't.

Lisa and her husband, Ross, are a perfect example of what happens when the only time a couple communicates is during television commercials.

Recently Lisa lamented to me about what it is like

for her, night after night, to stare at the vertical stripes on her family-room wallpaper while fantasizing about Clint Eastwood. Last week she heard Clint's voice more than her husband's. It was Clint Eastwood week on Channel 43. Noticing some of their preschooler's toys scattered around the room, Lisa began to collect them. Each time she walked in front of the TV Ross got more and more annoyed, until he finally said, "Would you please wait until the commercial comes on to do that?"

Lisa thought to herself, "Who are you kidding? What commercials? You channel-surf so much the sponsors could go out of business!" Lisa sat down and glared at the recliner Ross occupied, with its own special compartment for the remote control. She started plotting how to destroy the little black handheld demon. "I wonder if a trash-masher would kill it?" she mused. Then: "Lisa, get a grip on yourself!"

Her mind wandered back through their thirteen years of marriage. She vaguely remembered a time, before they had children, when they rarely turned on the television. Somehow the routine that accompanied child raising had paved the way for this nightly routine of television. Lisa was tired of Clint Eastwood. She wanted to hear her husband's voice. She decided to talk to Ross. Knowing the best time to get his attention was when he was channel-surfing, she waited for her chance. Her conversation with Ross went like this:

Lisa: I've been parent helper in Cassie's preschool class this week.

Ross *(still channel surfing):* Oh, good.

Lisa: Cassie's teacher asked me to come in to help get ready for the open house in two weeks.

Ross *(adjusting the recliner to a more horizontal position and quickly glancing at Lisa):* When is it?

Lisa: It's a week from Thursday at seven-thirty p.m. Will you be home in time for it?

Ross *(No response.)*

Lisa: Ross, are you listening?

Ross *(eyes still transfixed by the TV screen):* Yeah, I'm listening. What did you say?

Lisa: Oh, brother! Never mind. I'll tell you later.

Lisa watched Ross's eyes glaze over for another night. She could sit in front of the television for only so long before she felt compelled to do something, so finally she headed upstairs for a night of cleaning the linen closet.

If the only communication a couple has is at this surface level, they will soon become roommates. They may live under the same roof, share the same bathroom, and sleep in the same bed, but they will have no deep feelings of love and connection.

A Deeper Level

Life is too short to love this way, so let's put on our oxygen tanks and go down to the next level of communication. This is called *subsurface communication.* This is where couples share more than just surface information. They share ideas, opinions, and theories, and they intellectualize with each other. At this level, you'll find egos instead of fish! This is the level at which most arguments occur, because you have different opinions and ideas. If you can learn to appreciate those differences, then loving your mate will become natural and effortless.

Harry and Linda read the newspaper from front to back every Sunday and love to share their opinions on current events. Here is one of their typical conversations at the subsurface level:

Harry: That Tyson fight last night was great!

Linda: I thought it was crude and barbaric.

Harry: Hey, that's boxing. You've got to expect that.

Linda: Punching each other is one thing, but I think biting a piece of your opponent's ear off is out of control.

Harry: I don't think there's much difference between punching someone's face in and biting a chunk of his ear off.

Linda: At least punching someone requires skill. I think biting someone is just animalistic.

You can tell Harry and Linda are communicating on the subsurface level by their exchange of ideas and opinions and their use of the words "I think" to share their views.

Another couple, Pat and Joe, had differing opinions about the conviction of Timothy McVeigh in the Oklahoma bombing trial. Their conversation went like this:

Pat: I'm very pleased with the sentence for Timothy McVeigh. I think he deserves the death pen-
alty.

Joe: I think what he did was atrocious, but sentencing him to death doesn't help anyone.

Pat: Who cares if it helps anyone. I think he's a nut
case and should die for what he did.

Joe: I don't think it's right to take the life of someone even if they took the life of another.

Pat: I think it would be ridiculous to let this guy
off the hook. The families of those who died
need to see some action taken.

Joe: I think sentencing McVeigh to solitary confine-
ment for life is the action to take.

Michelle and Jim are both sports fanatics and love
to banter their opinions back and forth. Their Sunday
mornings are often spent around the kitchen table
with a cup of coffee and the sports page. A typical
conversation for them goes like this:

Michelle: I can't believe the Indians traded Kenny
Lofton to Atlanta. I think they're nuts.

Jim: I think the Indians got a pretty good deal with
Grissom and Justice.

Michelle: Neither of those guys can run like Lofton. I think Cleveland made a big mistake.

Jim: Honey, Justice is the one who hit the winning
home run against Cleveland in the World Series.

Michelle: So what! Lofton leads the league in most
bases stolen. I think he added more excitement
to the game than any Atlanta Brave.

None of these couples had an argument over the issues they were discussing. They simply shared their different opinions. Intellectual conversations can be stimulating in any relationship as long as one mate doesn't have to be right and the other wrong. Appreciating each other's opinions makes communicating on the subsurface level a rich and rewarding experience.

Going Deeper

We're going to turn up the oxygen now and go even deeper, down to the heart level. Here we descend into warm, clear tropical waters to experience magnificent reefs, soft corals, and exotic marine life of every color. When couples communicate on the heart level, they speak from their hearts instead of their heads. They use words like "I feel" rather than "I think." When expressing feelings of anger, frustration, or disappointment about something their mate has said or done, they do it by owning their feelings rather than blaming their mate for the way they feel.

Suppose your mate is two hours late for dinner. There are a couple of ways you can handle the situation:

- **Option #1:** You can explode when your mate walks through the door, saying, "Where have **you** been? How come **you** never let me know what's going on. **You** ruined my dinner and made me worry for the last two hours."
- **Option #2:** You can look at him or her with gen-

uine concern and say, "Thank God you're all right. When **I** didn't hear from you **I** was scared that something had happened to you. **I** felt so worried the whole time. Would you please call me right away when you know you'll be coming home late?

Notice that the first example uses the word "you" rather than "I." By approaching your mate this way, you pretty much set the stage for a juicy argument. By your second "you" sentence, your mate will already be gathering ammunition to defend her- or himself. In the second example, you focus on how **you** feel about your mate arriving home late. Then you ask briefly and directly for what you need.

Learning to talk on a feeling level, using statements that begin with "I feel . . ." rather than "You always . . ." may seem a lot like learning a new language, and it is. So to help you learn to communicate on a deep level effortlessly, I've created a simple four-step formula for you to follow:

Step 1. Describe the situation.
Step 2. Describe how the situation makes you feel.
Step 3. Ask for what you want, positively.
Step 4. Stop talking and give your mate a chance to respond.

One of the most common complaints I hear from women is that they can't get their husbands to stop reading the newspaper when they are talking to them. They plead, scream, bribe, and threaten with no success. One woman, Carol, described her dilemma one night in class. She said her conversations with her husband, Matt, went like this:

(Carol is talking to Matt while sitting at the kitchen table. Matt is reading the newspaper.)

Carol: Matt, you haven't heard a word I've said. Every time I want to talk to you, you're reading the newspaper. You never listen to me. All you do is stare at that dumb paper!

Matt *(still reading):* I'm listening. I'm listening.

Carol came to class one evening feeling triumphant. "I got him good this time," she said. "I canceled delivery!" I suggested she resubscribe to the newspaper and use my formula. She agreed, and the next time she found herself in that situation, here's what happened:

(Same scenario as before.)

Carol: Excuse me, honey, would you look at me for a minute?

(Matt puts the paper down and looks at his wife.)

Carol *(using Step 1):* Honey, when I see you reading the newspaper while I'm talking to you, *(Step 2)* I feel unimportant, like I don't matter as much as what's in the paper. *(Step 3)* I have something to talk to you about, so would you give me your attention for the next five minutes? I would really appreciate it.

(Step 4: Carol stops talking. She knows that if she goes on and on, she'll lose her husband's attention, and she has to give him a chance to respond.)

Matt *(folds the newspaper and places it on the table):* Go right ahead. I'm all ears.

For another couple, using the four-step formula made a huge difference in their marriage of fifteen years. Maggie was in the habit of launching into a recital of all the frustrations of her day the minute Bill came home from work. She would complain about the kids not cleaning their rooms, their daughter not practicing piano, or some contractor not showing up for a home-repair job. Bill would try to listen to her litany of complaints, but after a while he felt like he was carrying the weight of the world on his shoulders.

By using the four-step formula, Bill was able to share his feelings with Maggie and ask for what he needed. Here is what he said: "[Step 1] Maggie, when I come home at the end of the day, and I hear you venting your frustrations, [Step 2] I feel overwhelmed. [Step 3] I'd like to give you a ten-second kiss and then go upstairs for fifteen minutes to change my clothes and just decompress. Let's set time aside later in the evening to talk." Step 4: Bill stops talking and gives Maggie a chance to respond.

Maggie hadn't realized how her husband felt until he was able to express it this way. She honored his request, got a ten-second kiss, and got his full attention after he'd had a chance to shift gears. Bill got a ten-second kiss and some quiet time alone. It was a win-win situation.

Another student used the four-step formula to resolve a situation that had been bothering her for a long time. It angered Julianne that the only time her

husband ever brought up his desire to own a motorcycle was in a social setting. In front of everyone, Jeff
would say things like, "See, Julianne, everybody here
thinks I should get a motorcycle. What do you
think?"

They had several arguments about Jeff raising the
subject in the company of others. "By the time we
were done arguing about whether or not it was appropriate, we were too tired to make a decision about
the motorcycle," said Julianne.

I suggested that Julianne use the four-step formula
to share her feelings with Jeff. This is how she did it:

"[Step 1] Jeff, when we're with other people and
you bring up wanting a motorcycle and then ask me
what I think, [Step 2] I feel pressured and embarrassed. [Step 3] I would like you to keep our discussions about buying a motorcycle between just the two
of us." Step 4: Julianne stops talking and gives Jeff a
chance to respond.

Instead of feeling attacked, Jeff was able to listen to
Julianne's feelings, and he never brought up the subject in public again.

Another couple recounted their success story using the four-step formula. Cathy is a morning person.
She bounces out of bed and is immediately ready to
launch into a conversation. Rick is not a morning person. It takes him a couple of hours before he's ready
to interact with anyone. He wants nothing more than
to enjoy a long, hot shower in peace and solitude.
"The shower is where I do my creative thinking,"
says Rick. "I review my agenda for the day, plan my
strategy, and problem-solve while the water works
the kinks out of my body."

Early in their relationship, Cathy had developed a habit of poking her head into the bathroom and asking Rick questions while he was showering. Her inquiries ranged from confirming plans for that evening to telling him about her sister's new car. Cathy's morning visits to the bathroom really angered Rick, but he held his peace because he didn't want to get into an argument before going to work. When he learned about the four-step formula, he decided to try it:

"[Step 1] Cathy, when you ask me questions while I'm taking a shower, [Step 2] I feel invaded, like I have no privacy. [Step 3] I would like you to wait to talk to me until I'm in the kitchen and having my coffee." Step 4: Rick stops talking and gives Cathy a chance to respond.

Now Rick gets his privacy and Cathy knows she'll have his undivided attention at the breakfast table.

Remember Lisa, the woman who couldn't help fantasizing about Clint Eastwood because the only voice she heard in the evening was his? Well, she used the four-step formula and broke up the affair her husband was having with the remote control. Here is what she said:

"[Step 1] Ross, when I can't talk to you because your eyes are glued to the TV set, [Step 2] I feel like whatever you're watching is more important to you than I am. [Step 3]I'd like to turn off the set and talk to you for a half hour, three nights this week." Step 4: Lisa stops talking and gives Ross a chance to respond.

Now Lisa and Ross don't turn on the TV until they've had their thirty-minute talk. One night the TV never did get turned on. However, Ross did!

Whenever I get to the "Thirty-Minute Talk" portion of my lectures people look like they are going into cardiac arrest. I always get the same reaction. "Are you crazy? Thirty minutes without the television on? You want me to talk for thirty minutes?" You'd think I was asking them to disconnect their life-support system. "Yes, TV is addictive," I tell them. "You may go through withdrawal symptoms. Do it anyway. Break your addiction to the boob tube and get hooked on your mate instead."

Treasure Your Differences

Some of you reading this may be thinking, "That's great if you have a mate who likes to talk. But what if your mate is the silent type?" If you and your mate have different communication styles, it's no accident. Opposites attract. You may be more verbal. You like to give blow-by-blow descriptions of vacations, parties you've attended, movies you've seen, or dinners you've eaten. Your mate is less verbal, getting to the point with one-word adjectives like *fun, crowded, interesting,* or *tasty.*

You may be very open about your affairs, sharing your life with everyone. Your mate may be more private, feeling his or her life isn't anyone else's business.

You may talk first and think later. Your mate may be more cautious, mentally reviewing what he or she is going to say before speaking.

You may speak very loudly and forcefully. Your mate may tend to speak softly.

These are just differences in style. They are neither right nor wrong.

Earlier we talked about seeing your mate's traits in the same loving light as you did at the beginning of your relationship. When a couple first begins dating, there is usually no problem with conversation. In a new relationship, a couple pays no attention to who begins the conversation or who has more to talk about. What they notice is how comfortable they are with each other, how safe they feel telling each other things they've never shared before, or how they feel they've known each other all their lives. Whether your relationship is a year old or thirty years old, there is no reason why you can't feel the same way now.

Just remember the team concept and you'll be on the right track. You were attracted to your mate because of your differences. He or she had qualities you lacked. Together, you balance each other. Can you imagine if you and your mate were both verbal? You'd always be competing for airtime. On the other hand, if you were both the quiet type, the silence would drive you crazy.

If you are the more verbal partner, the responsibility for deepening your communication will probably be yours. Encourage your mate to speak more, and when he or she does speak . . . listen! If you're the quieter partner, push yourself to express your thoughts and ideas more often. Start small and watch for opportunities to state your opinion or express how you feel. Even if it's just deciding where to go for dinner, the quiet partner often tends to say, "I don't care," and let it go at that. Next time, say something like, "I really think it would be nice to eat by the water. How about that Chinese restaurant we used to go to? Does that sound good to you?" I'll bet you're thinking that's quite a mouthful—no pun intended—but you can do it!

I've seen countless examples of how partners with opposite communication styles can make a great team. One such couple are my friends Jack and Sandy. The following story, related to me by Sandy, demonstrates this point very well.

Sandy's father was having bypass surgery following a massive heart attack. Sandy and Jack were with Sandy's mother at the hospital. They had been in the waiting room for hours and were becoming anxious about the outcome, so Jack headed for the nurses' station to check on Sandy's dad's progress. While on his way there, he bumped into the surgeon who had just finished operating on Sandy's dad. Jack and the surgeon talked, and Jack returned to the waiting room to give his wife and mother-in-law the surgeon's report.

Jack entered the waiting room and said, "I just saw your dad's doctor. He's done with the surgery and said your dad is fine."

"What do you mean he's fine," said Sandy. "What else did he say?" Jack shrugged and said, "That's about it. He made it through the surgery and he'll be okay."

Sandy's jaw tensed as she hissed, "That can't be all the doctor said!"

At that moment, Sandy's mother began to sob with relief. She walked over to Jack, hugged him, and said, "Oh, thank God he's going to be okay."

Jack's short-but-sweet report of his father-in-law's

condition was all Sandy's mother needed to hear. The details were unimportant. From that moment on Sandy had a new appreciation for her husband's less verbal communication style.

One of my students volunteered this story in class one night when I was talking about differences in communication style. Mark said he used to complain that his wife, Barb, was too talkative, until he saw her in action one Saturday afternoon. They were driving home from a trip to the supermarket. As they waited in line to make a left turn, the car in front of them turned left into oncoming traffic. They watched in horror as the car was hit broadside by another car traveling at a good clip. After the crash, Mark and Barb jumped out of their car and ran to the scene of the accident. Seeing that the driver who had been broadsided was bleeding badly from his head, Mark ran to use his car phone and call an ambulance. He was stunned by what he saw when he returned to the injured man. His wife was sitting in the bloodied front seat of the mangled car and was talking nonstop to the driver, who was fading in and out of consciousness. Barb's ongoing conversation kept him awake until the rescue squad arrived.

"I could never have done what Barb did," said Mark. "The guy would have slipped into a coma if he'd had to depend on me to keep him awake."

If your mate is the silent type and you're the talker, your understanding and appreciation of your differences will be an important factor in improving your communication with each other. As the talker, it will be up to you to encourage your mate by talking less and listening more.

Diving for Treasure

Now that you've learned to share with your mate at the heart level and to appreciate his or her style of communication, you are ready to turn up your oxygen tanks and descend at last to the ocean floor. Here is where you'll find the most precious treasure of all— a gift to give to each other that will enrich and deepen your relationship beyond your wildest dreams. I'm talking about the gift of listening.

When you truly listen to your mate, you give him or her the gift of your time, your attention, your open mind, and your open heart. Real listening is an art form, and being a good listener usually doesn't come naturally. In fact, as children we were often taught *not to* listen by adults who frequently didn't listen to us. Can you remember repeating "Mommy, Mommy" over and over again—trying in vain to get Mom's attention? Or saying, "I'm scared," or "I'm hurt," and getting an inappropriate response? Instead of hearing, "I know how frightening that must be," or "That must really hurt, ouch!" we were told, "Don't be silly. There's nothing to be afraid of," or "Stop acting like a baby. That doesn't hurt." Eventually we got the message. Nobody's listening!

If the adults in our lives had done a better job of listening to us, we would be better listeners ourselves. Many of today's parents are very conscientious about showing their children they're listening by acknowledging their feelings. For example, a student in one of my classes recalls the time her son needed an injection of antibiotics to fight a serious infection. The nurse walked into the examining room holding a syringe with an enormous needle attached to it and said to Sarah's six-year-old, "Now, this isn't going to hurt."

Sarah looked at the nurse and said, "Who are you kidding? Of course it's going to hurt!" She asked the nurse to step out of the room for a few minutes. Her son had already climbed down from the examining table and was crouched in the corner of the room crying, "I'm scared, Mommy. Is it gonna hurt? I'm scared."

Sarah knelt down next to her son and said, "I know you're scared, honey. You've never had a shot like this before. It's going to hurt for a couple of seconds, but then it won't hurt anymore."

Satisfied that his mom had listened to him and given him an honest response, Sean bravely climbed back onto the examining table and took the shot without protest.

It's obvious Sarah's a good listener, but was she always? The answer is no. Sarah learned to become a good listener because she wanted to be a good parent. You can learn to be a good listener, too, by using the steps shown below. You'll know you are truly listening to your mate when you:

1. Give your mate your full attention by looking at him or her.
2. Don't interrupt your mate except to ask a question in order to better understand what he or she is saying.
3. Repeat back to your mate what you think he or she is saying.
4. Don't judge, criticize, or minimize your mate's problem.

5. Assume that your mate doesn't want your advice unless he or she asks for it.

If you can practice these five steps when your mate is talking, you will be listening from your heart. If, while your mate is talking, you find yourself thinking of ways to help him or her solve the problem, or how you're going to respond, then you're not listening! You should put on your "Fix It Hat" only when your mate says he or she wants your advice. By not giving unsolicited advice, we are telling our partner that we have faith in their ability to solve their own problems.

Debbie, a freelance writer, was shocked when, out of the blue, the newspaper she had been writing for pulled her weekly column. When her husband, Rob, came home that night, he found Debbie very upset. Rob had a big opportunity to listen to Debbie with his heart, but he put on his "Fix It Hat" and missed his opportunity. Their conversation went like this:

Rob: Deb, what's the matter?

Debbie *(starting to cry):* I can't believe it. My editor called today and told me that last week's column would be my final one.

Rob: You're kidding!

Debbie: I'm in shock. It's like I'm here today, gone tomorrow.

Rob: Did you ask him why your column got cut?

Debbie: He said the section wasn't getting enough advertising, so they had to cut several features. My column was one of them.

Rob: Why don't you call him back and see if he'll let you write once a month.

Debbie: I don't want to write once a month. I want my weekly column back!

Rob: Why don't you try writing for a community newspaper. I'm sure they'd be interested in your work.

Debbie: I don't want to write for any other newspaper.

Rob: How about magazines?

Debbie *(going upstairs):* I just want to be alone.

Rob forgot two of the most important rules of listening. He didn't empathize and reflect Debbie's feelings back to her, and he gave her advice when she wasn't asking for it. This could have been an opportunity for them to connect on a heart level and get a piece of the treasure. If they had done that, here is what their conversation would have sounded like:

Rob: Deb, what's the matter?

Debbie *(starting to cry):* I can't believe it. My editor called today and told me that last week's column would be my final one.

Rob: You're kidding!

Debbie: I'm in shock. It's like I'm here today, gone tomorrow.

Rob: You're feeling pretty dispensable, huh?

Debbie: Yeah. *(Starting to cry again.)*

Rob: Oh, honey, come here. *(Putting his arms around her.)* I'm so sorry this happened.

Debbie: I just don't understand how a newspaper can pull a popular column like that.

Rob: It's pretty aggravating to have people making decisions that affect what you love to do.

Debbie: I feel like I have absolutely no control.

Rob: That must feel awful.

Debbie: It does.

Rob: You're a terrific writer and your column is outstanding. I'm sorry this happened.

Debbie: Oh, honey. Thanks for being my biggest fan.

Debbie felt closer to Rob because he really listened to what she was saying and then validated her feelings.

Most of the time your mate won't want your advice. He or she will just want to vent and know that you're there to listen. One of my students told me that before she and her second husband got married, she explained exactly that concept to him. "In my first marriage, my husband always wanted to fix whatever problem I was having. Somehow, his advice always made me feel like he thought I was a child. I know a lot of men have trouble just listening, that they think they need to do something, so I decided to explain to Al that unless I asked for advice, all I wanted was his arms around me, and his caring attention. I guess he was listening, because we've been together fifteen years, and his arms and his heart are always open when I come to him with a problem. But unless I specifically ask him, he never offers advice."

Nip It in the Bud

In any long-term committed relationship, there will be plenty of days when something your mate does will irk you, offend you, or really tick you off. Welcome to the world of human relations! When this happens, you can either ignore it, shove it under the rug and wait for it to rear its ugly head later, or you can address it, face it, and nip it in the bud.

How many times have you and your mate argued over some dumb thing that has nothing to do with what is really bothering you? This happens all the time. And it's usually because couples think the problem will either go away or work itself out. Instead, what starts out as a minor irritation turns into a major resentment and often a hurtful argument.

I witnessed a perfect example of this not long ago while at a curbside baggage check-in line at the airport. As I turned to lift and carry my bags a few inches, I noticed a family of four behind me. What caught my attention was the mother struggling to push a double stroller with a diaper bag on her arm, while trying to put a ponytail in her daughter's hair. The father stood with a golf bag balanced on one shoulder and a suitcase in his other hand.

A few seconds later, I heard a bloodcurdling scream. Several of us in line turned to find the mother behind me practically scalping her toddler as she brushed her hair into a ponytail. After about five minutes of the little girl yelling, "Don't do my hair, Mommy," the father calmly looked at his wife and said, "Do you have to do that now?" Totally exasperated, the mother finally gave up.

I stood there remembering our children's toddler days. I thought to myself, "I give her a lot of credit for traveling by plane with two little ones." As I turned around to give her an admiring look, I saw her poised with the brush in her hand, ready to dive into her daughter's hair once more. I noticed the looks on the surrounding faces as she prepared for the second attack. We were all thinking the same thing: "Aw, lady, no. Don't do it. Not again. Pleeeease!" Sure enough, there followed another round of screams.

After a while I began to think this mother's mission to put her daughter's hair in a ponytail was more than just a matter of grooming. Behind the hairdresser facade was the face of an angry woman. The question was, What had made this woman so upset with her daughter that she would put her through such torture? Then it happened. The source of all the anger and frustration finally spewed out as I heard the following conversation between the husband and wife:

> Wife: This hasn't been a vacation for me. I watched you go play golf with your father every day while I stayed home with the kids.
>
> Husband: That wasn't my intention.
>
> Wife: That may not have been your intention, but that's what happened. It happens every time we go see your parents. Your father always takes you golfing while I stay home. I'm sick and tired of going on vacation and baby-sitting while you play.
>
> Husband (*staring off into space*): I'm sorry you feel that way.

Although I didn't know all the details of this couple's background, one thing was clear to me. While the woman in this situation may have been frustrated about her daughter's hair, she was really angry at her husband. Unfortunately, her daughter took the brunt of her wrath. This poor lady's anger had probably been building up all week long, maybe even since the last trip to her in-laws'. This couple's conflict is a classic case of what happens in so many relationships. Negative feelings build up, and if not addressed right away they turn into major resentments. Sadly enough, there are couples who hang on to their resentments so long that they no longer care about resolving them.

The next time you're tempted to ignore something that seriously annoys you, remember these four pointers on how to nip it in the bud:

1. If something in your relationship is bothering you for more than two minutes, address it with your mate.
2. Avoid taking your anger out on an innocent bystander, such as a child or co-worker, by handling the situation right away.
3. Timing is everything. If you wait to discuss a problem until long after the fact, chances are you will find yourself "losing it" at an inappropriate place, like the baggage check-in line at the airport.
4. When you express your concerns to your mate at the time they occur, he or she will be more willing to listen. If you hit him or her with a long angry monologue of issues built up over time, your partner will most likely "go away" in mind, if not in body.

Don't forget to nip it in the bud, and you'll go a long way toward keeping your relationship something special.

The K.I.S.S. Plan

To take care of yourself, you spend time every day sleeping, eating, breathing, and relaxing. These are all things you must do to stay healthy—your body requires it. And, to stay healthy, your relationship requires daily care and attention. **K**eep **I**t **S**omething **S**pecial with a thirty-minute talk each day and your relationship will thrive.

I want you to carve thirty minutes out of your schedule every day to spend talking with your mate. I don't care if you talk while you walk, talk while you drive, or talk while you sit by the fire. When or where you talk doesn't matter. What counts is that you do it!

If you are used to communicating only on the surface level, then start there. If, for the first several times you have a thirty-minute talk, you can't get past talking about "stuff" like who'll take the car in for service, when your mother is coming to dinner, or the date of your daughter's open house, that's okay. Sharing information is better than not sharing at all.

Little by little, start to share your opinions. Just make sure you allow each other to have different ones. By taking a genuine interest in each other's ideas, you'll be surprised at how much you'll learn about the both of you. Talk about anything—current events, religion, politics, community issues. The sky is the limit.

During your time together, share at least one feeling about something. Get into the habit of sharing from your heart as well as your head. You might feel vulnerable making this intimate connection on a daily basis, but for trust to build in your relationship, you have to do it.

Listen to your mate when he or she is talking. During your thirty-minute talk, keep distractions to a minimum. Close off the outside world by turning off the television, turning off the ringer on your phone, and closing your bedroom door if you need to.

4

THE
TWENTY-SECOND
HUG

Touching for All Ages

It's common knowledge that touching feels good. Whether you are the one touching or the one being touched, physical contact with another person feeds the soul. From the moment we draw our first breath to the moment we take our last, we crave being touched.

You see this powerful need in babies who nuzzle against their mother's neck or settle into their father's arms. According to an article that appeared in the August 1997 issue of *Life* magazine, entitled "The Magic Touch," by George Howe Colt, touch can even be a matter of life and death. This fact, which was inadvertently discovered in the thirteenth century, has been confirmed many times since then, most recently in Romania during the early 1990s. Thousands of infants were warehoused in orphanages, and left virtually untouched in their cribs for two years. Those that survived were found to be severely impaired.

On the other hand, babies who are touched flourish. At the Touch Research Institute in Miami, premature babies who were massaged three times a day for ten days were found to be more alert, active, and responsive than babies who weren't massaged. They were able to sleep more deeply, gained weight forty-seven percent faster, and were released from the hospital six days sooner.

Even the most casual touch can yield surprising results. For example, waitresses who touch their customers on the hand or shoulder as they return change receive bigger tips than those who don't.

It's very apparent how important touch is to school-age children. Little girls walk around holding hands or with their arms around each other. Little boys need touch too, but because in America tender touching among males is socially taboo, they jab, punch, and shove each other instead. They may not realize it, but they horse around because they want the physical contact.

Studies have shown that children whose parents hug, tickle, and touch them are happier and more social and have fewer adjustment problems than children raised by parents who don't touch them much. Research also shows that these same children grow up to have closer friendships and happier marriages than the children who weren't given physical affection by their parents. In addition, cultures that show more physical affection toward infants and children tend to have lower rates of adult violence.

In families where parents don't touch their children, it only stands to reason that the siblings in the family also don't touch each other affectionately. Rebecca, a woman in my *Light His Fire* class, was raised in a very undemonstrative family. In class one evening, she told us about one of the rare times her brother touched her affectionately.

"I was sixteen years old," said Rebecca. "It was midnight on a Saturday night a few weeks after my brother Dale's wedding to his childhood sweetheart, Carla. I was awakened by the sound of the phone ringing. I heard my father answer it and say, 'Oh my God. We'll be right there.'

"I instinctively bolted out of bed and asked my father who had called. 'It was the hospital. Dale and Carla have been in a car accident.' My parents and I threw on our clothes and sped to the hospital, not even stopping for red lights. We were met in emergency by a nurse who asked if we were Dale's family.'

" 'Yes,' we said.

" 'I'm so sorry,' she responded.

" 'Sorry for what? What are you sorry for?' we asked.

"The nurse led us into a small room. 'Your son is hurt, but he'll be okay,' she told us. 'I'm so sorry, but his wife is gone.'

"In the same instant that we felt relieved that Dale was alive, we felt devastated that Carla was dead.

"The next few days were a nightmare, telling Dale he had lost his bride of six weeks, making funeral arrangements, going through the memorial service. Many of the details I've forgotten. But I do remember this. The day of the funeral there was a gathering for family and friends at my parents' house. Dale and I were sitting next to each other on the patio, talking with some of the guests, when suddenly Dale took my hand in his. I was amazed. I remember thinking, 'He's holding my hand. My brother, who has never touched me affectionately in any way, shape, or form, is holding my hand.' We sat like that, hand in hand, for several minutes and for the very first time, I knew my brother loved me. I thanked God he was alive."

Please Touch

Sadly, in today's world, children hungry for touch can't even count on it in school. With growing concerns about sexual harassment and abuse in schools, touch has become taboo, even in preschool. This taboo is reflected in the slogan "Teach, don't touch". That's why it warmed my heart so when I heard recently of a teaching assistant who is well known in school and in her community for the hugs she gives her students. The kids call her "Aunt Rose."

Aunt Rose is seventy-eight years old and has been a teaching assistant for first graders for the last twelve years. The children's regular teacher teaches the children reading, writing, and arithmetic. Aunt Rose teaches them love. She says, "I can't tell you how many times I'll be helping a child with math or reading and he or she will look up at me with big eyes and say, 'Aunt Rose, can I have a hug?' I have twelve years' worth of cards from children thanking me for hugging them."

Teenagers want to be touched just as much as younger children do. They pretend to be cool and distant, but underneath that "don't you dare touch me" attitude is a kid dying for a big bear hug. This "cool" denial of the need to be touched is not universal, however. French teenagers are much more physically demonstrative than American teens. Casual touching, such as leaning on a friend or putting an arm around another's shoulder, is a matter of course for them. Psychologist Tiffany Field, the director of Miami's Touch Research Institute, has found that French parents and children touch one another three times more frequently than their American counterparts, regardless of their age.

In one of my classes a student named Frank told a story that brought tears to everyone's eyes. Frank had admitted to not being very demonstrative with his children, especially his teenage son. As he explained it, his dad hadn't touched him much when he was growing up, so of course he tended to keep his distance with his own son. The week after we talked about touching in the men's class, Frank came in and told us what had happened between him and his son during the week. Frank owned a carpet company, and his teenage son, Rob, often helped him cut carpet at night.

"One night last week, Rob and I were in the warehouse cutting a piece of white carpeting for a customer," said Frank. "I noticed Rob had a can of cola on the floor next to the carpet we were cutting. No sooner had I said, 'Rob, move the can so it doesn't spill,' than he knocked it over and spilled the soda all over the white carpet. Normally, I would have gone into a rage. I'm pretty hard on Rob. I usually don't cut him a lot of slack, but because of what I've learned in this class I reacted differently this time. Rob knew he had made a careless mistake and he started apologizing and even started to tremble in fear, anticipating my wrath.

"Instead of yelling, I calmly said, 'That's okay, Rob. We'll clean it up.' He didn't even hear me. He just kept apologizing, on the verge of tears. So, for the first time in my life as a father, I walked over to him, gave him a big hug, and said, 'Son, it's okay.' We stood there embracing for a long time. We both had tears running down our cheeks as that hug helped us release feelings of love we had never shared before. Rob and I have a different relationship now, and it feels wonderful."

As children, we desperately want to be touched, and although we may deny it, the yearning for physical contact doesn't disappear just because we're adults. No matter how much we proclaim, "I'm not the huggy-kissy type," deep down we want to be hugged, held, caressed, and stroked. Touch is the first sense to develop in humans, and it may be the last to fade.

Ruth offered this story when we talked about touching in class. She had just participated in a workshop for volunteers at her church. The day was packed with small-group activities designed to develop teamwork.

"I was bored and restless during the workshop until we ended the day with an exercise called the Angel Walk," Ruth said. She explained that the Angel Walk started with people forming two lines facing each other.

"One by one, the minister instructed each of us to

close our eyes, stretch our arms out in front of us, and walk down between the two lines of people. He then instructed the people in the lines to touch the person walking down the middle and whisper something in his or her ear.

"I watched men and women ranging in age from thirty to seventy-five walk down the middle of the aisle having their hands touched, their shoulders rubbed, and their heads stroked. By the time each of us had done the Angel Walk, we were all emotionally moved, some of us to tears," said Ruth. "You could see in our faces how much being touched affected us."

A Touch for All Reasons

If being touched by strangers can be so moving, can you imagine how important being touched by your mate is? It doesn't matter how far apart you may have grown in your relationship; you can all recall a time when your mate's touch comforted you, calmed you, or sexually excited you. Whenever I ask students to share ways that their mate's touch has affected them, I always get plenty of people ready to respond.

For example, Joyce related how her husband, Jay, comforted her the day her father died. Joyce was with her mother at the hospital when her father died unexpectedly during routine surgery. According to the surgeon, her dad's blood pressure had plummeted and they had been unable to save him.

"It was such a shock," said Joyce. "I remember

falling apart completely and thinking how much I wanted Jay with me.

"Jay headed for the hospital as soon as he heard the news, and within minutes he walked in and wrapped his big strong arms around me. I was sobbing so hard I was hyperventilating. As he held me close to his chest, I could feel the rhythm of his breathing. Very soon Jay and I were inhaling and exhaling in sync and I was breathing normally again."

According to another student, his girlfriend's touch was healing. Todd suffered from chronic sinus headaches, and no amount of inhalers, decongestants, or vaporizers could equal what his girlfriend, Christine, could do with her fingertips. "Christine knows the exact way to press on my forehead to relieve my headache," said Todd.

Liz told me how she looked forward every night to lying in bed next to her husband as he lightly stroked her arms. "It's wonderful," said Liz. "No matter what kind of day I have, I know I'll be able to release my stress when Dennis 'does my arms.' For Christmas, he bought me a beautiful, big peacock feather to use on my arms, but I told him nothing can replace his touch."

Unfortunately, many of the couples I talk to experience what I call "skin hunger." They stop touching for some reason—perhaps they've had a big fight or they've let a lot of small issues go unresolved. A few days turn into a week, weeks turn into months, and eventually the couple realizes they haven't touched each other in a year. They may still be sexual with each other, but that's not the kind of touching I'm talking about. I'm talking about nonsexual touching, such as hugging, rubbing, stroking, and caressing.

One student, Tony, reminisced with me about how much he missed the kind of affectionate touching he and his wife enjoyed before they had kids. Every night after dinner, Tony would stretch out on the sofa and lie with his head in Charlotte's lap as she caressed his forehead. "We have three children now," said Tony. "Charlotte's lap has been the resting place for our children instead of my head for the last twelve years."

Ted, a man in one of my *Light Her Fire* classes, shared a technique he and his wife had learned at a Marriage Encounter weekend years before. They had used it successfully to stay connected, even during their child-rearing days. "Once a week, we do a 'skin-to-skin,'" said Ted. According to Ted, a "skin-to-skin" means that when it's bedtime, he and his wife lie wrapped in each other's arms, naked, and fall asleep that way. "The presenter at the Marriage Encounter weekend wanted us to learn to enjoy touching each other's bodies without intercourse being the goal," said Ted. "I have to admit this was a tough one for me at first. But I quickly learned to enjoy the feeling of Shirley's body next to me, without any expectations. Whenever we do this, we feel closer to each other. The next time we make love is always especially satisfying."

The need for touch does not diminish with age. Unfortunately, many older people suffer from severe touch deprivation. They've lost their mate, and they live lonely lives with little outside contact. Given the opportunity to touch and be touched on a regular basis proved to be very beneficial to elders in another study done by the Touch Research Institute. Volunteers over the age of sixty were given three weeks of massage and trained to massage toddlers. These seniors were less depressed, had lower stress levels, and were less lonely than before they began the study. They also had fewer doctor visits and were more socially active.

Mr. and Mrs. Campbell, a couple in their eighties, still love to touch each other. They share a room in the nursing home where Elaine, a woman in one of my classes, worked as a housekeeper.

"My favorite room to clean was always Mr. and Mrs. Campbell's," said Elaine. "It just tickled me to see how much they touched each other."

Elaine told us that one day she would see them sitting next to each other holding hands. Another day she would walk in to see Mrs. Campbell rubbing lotion on Mr. Campbell's legs. More than once, she walked in to find Mr. Campbell brushing Mrs. Campbell's hair.

"I've heard that married couples live longer than people who live alone," said Elaine. "At the rate the Campbells are going, they'll be celebrating their 110th birthdays together."

When Opportunity Knocks, Open the Door

No matter how busy or hectic your daily life is, there are always opportunities to touch your mate. Look at the list below and see if you recognize any opportunities you've missed.

■ **Rubbing your feet against your mate's legs as you lie next to each other in bed.**

Catherine loved to get into bed with her husband, Jeff, and run her feet up and down his legs. "The hair on his legs is so soft, and his legs are so warm," said Catherine. "I love it especially during winter, when my feet are freezing."

"It's a bit of a jolt in the winter," said Jeff, "but it's a small price to pay to stay close to my sweetheart."

■ **Touching your mate's shoulder while he or she is reading.**

Married for forty-two years, both Kate and Jonathan love to curl up with a good book on Sunday afternoons. "Sometimes I'll garden while Jon is reading or Jon will work in the basement while I'm reading," says Kate. "We have an understanding that if a big portion of the afternoon has gone by without us talking to each other, the one who isn't reading will check in on the other."

"I can get so engrossed in reading the latest best-seller that I forget about everything," adds Jonathan. "It's nice to feel Kate's hand on my shoulder to let me know she's around and wondering how I'm doing."

■ **Hugging your mate while he or she is doing the dishes.**

Deborah and Simon share housework. "Simon cooks and I wash the dishes," says Deborah. "Although washing dishes is one of my least favorite chores, there's a big payoff in it for me."

Every night when Deborah is up to her elbows in soapsuds, her husband slips his arms around her waist. "He starts by giving me a hug from behind and then gently kisses my neck. The kissing usually turns to nibbling. On the evenings when Simon holds me tight and kisses the back of my ear, I throw in the towel and the dishes don't get done until morning."

■ **Holding your mate's hand while walking or driving.**

Bill and Gretchen recently bought a new car, and their decision of what kind to get showed me that they really put their relationship first.

"When we went car shopping, we both fell in love with a little red Fiat," said Bill. "It had everything we wanted—electric windows, leather seats, a CD player—but we didn't get it. It had one major drawback. It was a stick shift."

Gretchen and Bill love to hold hands while driving, and a stick shift cramps their style. Now, that's keeping your priorities straight.

■ **Putting your head or your feet in your partner's lap while watching TV.**

Mary and Ted don't watch much TV, but when they do, they try to stay connected. "We got into a rut for a while," said Mary. "Ted sat in his recliner and I sat on the couch. After an evening of staring at the boob tube, we were oblivious to each other. We started to feel more and more distance between us and couldn't figure out why. Ted came up with the idea to touch each other while watching TV."

"Now we sit on the couch together and one of us will put our head or feet in the other's lap," said Ted. "It's hard to ignore someone when they're rubbing your feet or stroking your forehead. We feel close again, and watching TV has become much more enjoyable!"

■ **Playing "footsie" with your mate under the table when you're at a restaurant.**

Lee's job as a salesman requires him and his wife, Cindy, to take clients to dinner several times a week. "I know entertaining clients is important to Lee's career, but it gets tiresome at times," says Cindy. "So to spice things up a little, Lee and I play footsie under the dinner table."

Cindy is usually the one to begin their foot connection. "I start by tapping Lee's shoe, then I run my leg up and down his calf. It's fun to watch him try to concentrate on the conversation while I'm rubbing his leg under the table."

"I normally like it when Cindy rubs my leg with her foot," adds Lee. "There was this one time, though, when her shoe fell off, and I had to crawl under the table to get it. My client thought it was hilarious."

■ **Connecting during a ride in an empty elevator.**

Whenever Dorothy and her husband step into an empty elevator, a little grin spreads across their faces.

"We make it a game," says Dorothy. "As soon as the elevator doors close, we embrace, kiss, and touch each other wherever we want to. It's so exciting to know that we only have a certain amount of time to do this. Merv gets nervous when we get into an elevator that doesn't ding when the door opens. I love it. No ding makes it more exciting!"

Couples who are in the habit of touching have no trouble finding opportunities. Even in the hustle and bustle of everyday life, loving couples can find a way to touch. Vicki and her husband, Bruce, spend most of their summer evenings at a ball field, since Bruce is the first-base coach for their son's Little League team.

They don't let the chain-link fence separate them, though. "I make sure I come over to the stands and give Vicki a kiss or a neck rub in between innings," says Bruce. Vicki recalls a couple of games when Bruce had to be umpire. "The poor guy was stuck out on the field the whole game," she says. "But whenever a new pitcher came in and practiced a few throws with the catcher, Bruce and I would 'touch base' at the fence and talk, touching each other's fingers through the holes."

May I Have This Dance?

Dancing with your mate affords you a fabulous opportunity to touch each other. Unfortunately, either the man, the woman, or both partners sometimes feel self-conscious getting on the dance floor.

Andy and Felecia, who both took my classes, told me how dancing renewed their relationship. Twenty-four years ago, Felecia and Andy were on their honeymoon in Old San Juan, Puerto Rico. Dressed elegantly, they sat in a restaurant that was oozing with romantic ambience. The Latin rhythms the band played had them tapping their feet as they enjoyed their meal and watched the couples on the dance floor doing the samba, the rumba, and the cha-cha. They had the following conversation while sitting at the table:

Felecia (*shyly looking at Andy*): Do you want to dance?

Andy (*clearly uncomfortable, but pretending to be excited*): Sure! (Praying she'll say no.) Do you?

Felecia: I'd love to, but I don't know how to dance this way. Do you?

Andy (*with a sigh of relief*): No. I wouldn't have the slightest idea how to begin. Look at them! How do they get their hips to move like that?

Felecia: I don't know, but I sure would love to learn someday.

Andy: Me too.

Well, that "someday" didn't come for Andy and Felecia until many years later. For the first twenty-one years of their marriage, they sat as spectators at wedding receptions and anniversary parties while other couples enjoyed dancing with each other. Then three years ago, something happened that motivated Felecia and Andy to finally take dance lessons. Felecia's mother, who herself loved to dance, was told she had to have her foot amputated. Three weeks before her mother's operation, Felecia felt a strong tug at her heart. She realized there was no guarantee that something like this might not happen to her or Andy someday. She knew the time had come for them to learn to dance, and they enrolled in a beginners' ballroom dance class.

At first, she and Andy were nervous, but after six months of dance lessons, they felt proficient enough to dance anywhere. Looking back on it, Felecia and Andy say that dancing has been the best thing they've ever done for their marriage. "We not only learned how to dance, we learned how to touch each other again," said Felecia.

"We used to be the first to leave a wedding reception," said Andy. "Now we don't go home till the band does."

The Hugs Have It

Of all the ways there are to touch, hugging is probably the top choice. We hug in times of joy, sorrow, elation, pride, forgiveness, and even pain. Although not practiced as often in America as in other countries, the hug is a universal language. Regardless of race or nationality, a hug says, "I care about you."

Unfortunately, in our American society, a stigma surrounds hugging. Somewhere along the line, a lot of us picked up the message that it's not manly for men to hug each other. If a woman hugs a man, she has an ulterior motive. If a father hugs his son, he'll make him a sissy. None of these ideas could be further from the truth. A hug is a way to let another person know you care, regardless of whether that person is male or female, adult or child.

There is one place, however, where hugging happens regularly without shame or embarrassment. Sadly, that place is a funeral home.

"I was in a fog during calling hours at my father's wake," one woman told me. "I remember faces coming close to mine, one at a time, and people saying the standard lines, 'I'm so sorry,' 'He's in heaven now,' 'The pain will go away with time,' or 'He wasn't himself at the end. It's better this way.' As well meaning as their words were, they actually gave me little or no comfort.

"What got me through those days and nights before the funeral were the people who came up to me, said nothing, and just hugged me. Through their embraces, I received the love and strength I needed to carry on."

A hug not given can be as powerful as one that is. A hug that is desperately craved but withheld can leave a negative memory that lasts forever. I felt Nanette's pain when she told me that was exactly what happened to her.

"I had the lead role in a community theater production," said Nanette. "My parents were in the front row during one of the shows, and I could hear my father laughing after many of my lines. It made me so happy that he liked my performance.

"My parents had agreed to meet me at a nearby restaurant after the show. When I walked into the restaurant, my father sauntered up to me with an approving look on his face. I wanted so much for him to hug me, but instead he stuck out his hand and said,

'Nice job.' I plastered a fake smile on my face and thanked him. I could have been handed a Tony award and it wouldn't have canceled the pain I felt at that moment. All I wanted was for my daddy to hug me. When I walked into that restaurant, I was excited and full of life. When my father shook my hand instead of hugging me, I felt like he had shaken the life right out of me."

There is no question that touching sustains life. Research indicates that receiving hugs significantly increases the supply of oxygen to all the organs in our bodies. Even a simple touch can reduce the heart rate and lower the blood pressure. Touch also stimulates the release of endorphins, the body's natural pain suppressors. The healing touch of massage boosts immune function, improves the ability to concentrate, lowers anxiety, and has been shown to have positive effects on colic, hyperactivity, diabetes, and migraines. Instinctively, we've known for ages that touch is life-enhancing. When Michelangelo painted God extending a hand toward Adam on the ceiling of the Sistine Chapel, he chose touch to depict the gift of life.

The power of touch can also help release a life, as demonstrated in the following story related to me by Amanda.

When Annie, Amanda's mom, was diagnosed with lung cancer and told she had three months to live, Amanda vowed to spend every day with her mother. She watched helplessly as the cancer spread from her mother's lung to her hip, and finally to her brain. "There was nothing I could do except help her get ready to die," mourned Amanda.

"One night I decided to go to a movie with my husband. I had been with my mom all day and needed a break. After the movie, I saw signs posted all over the lobby for me to call home. I knew it was time for my mom to go. My husband rushed me to Mom's house. When I walked in, the nurse explained that Mom had spiked a high fever. The nurse felt this indicated that she didn't have long, but during the next hour Mom's temperature went back to normal. I was tired and decided to go home. However, as I was getting ready to leave I had this unusual feeling that I should stay. I told my husband to go on home without me and that I'd see him the next day.

"About an hour after my husband left, my mom's breathing became very labored. The hospice nurse told me she thought my mom was getting ready to leave. 'Oh, my God,' I said. 'What can I do? I wish I could get into bed with her and just hug her.'

" 'Then do it,' the nurse replied softly.

"I quickly took off my shoes, got into bed, and wrapped my arms around my mother's wasted body. I held her close to my heart and whispered in her ear how much I loved her and how much God loved her. As I looked into her eyes and said, 'I'm handing you over to God now, Mom,' she took her last breath.

"This dear woman had brought me into this world. I'm so blessed that I was able to help her leave it with a loving embrace."

To Hug Me Is to Love Me

"Hug me," "I need a hug," "Give me a hug," "Can I have a hug?" "Do you need a hug?" "Would you like a hug?" "How about a hug?" What man or woman in any loving relationship has not uttered one of these phrases to another? The arms of your mate can be a refuge, a sanctuary, a safe haven to run to when you need to know you are cared about.

Unfortunately, couples can find dozens of reasons not to hug. Here's one I had never thought about until Sandy shared a story with me about why she and her husband didn't hug. "I'm five feet, two inches tall and Walter is six foot four. Hugging was always very awkward and uncomfortable. Walter would have to hunch over me and I'd have to crane my neck so far back, I'd feel like I was in the first row of a movie theater. Finally, we agreed to forget trying to hug each other, until I took *Light His Fire*. When you talked about the importance of hugging I decided we needed to find a way to hug again. I figured out that if Walter stood at the foot of the stairs and I stood on the second step, we'd be about the same height. We tried it that night after class, and it worked! After hugging, Walter looked at me with a tear in his eye and said, 'That was wonderful. I've really missed hugging you.' Now we can hug comfortably any time we feel like it."

I guess, if you think about it long enough, you can always find a reason not to hug your mate. So, to show you how easy it is to find a reason to hug your mate on a daily basis, I've included the following list:

17 Reasons to Hug Your Mate
 1. For no reason at all.
 2. To say "Thank you."
 3. To say "Hello."
 4. To say "Good-bye."
 5. To say "Good night."
 6. To say "Good morning."
 7. To say "Happy birthday."
 8. To say "I'm sorry."
 9. To say "I'm proud of you."
10. To say "Congratulations."
11. To say "I know it's scary."
12. To say "We won!"
13. To say "I know it hurts."
14. To say "You're my hero."
15. To say "I love you."
16. To say "I'll protect you."
17. To say "You make me laugh."

A hug is always wonderful, but some hugs are more significant than others and become part of a memorable event. For example, Hank told me a story about the time a hug kept his wife from going over the edge.

"It was a late summer's afternoon a couple of years ago," said Hank. "Marcia and I had left work early to go sailing. We took along a picnic dinner, some romantic music, and a bottle of wine. Two hours into our little getaway, I noticed some dark clouds rolling in. Within a few short minutes the weather report had changed from 'sunny and light winds' to a storm watch. I told Marcia we would have to turn back right away. I don't know how it happened so quickly, but before I could get us pointed in the right direction, we were surrounded by seven-to-twelve foot waves. I tried to gain control of our craft, but we kept going in circles, lurching from one wave to the next.

"I remember Marcia screaming hysterically, 'Oh my God, what do we do?' I threw her a life jacket and told her to go below. I grabbed onto anything sturdy to be able to make my way to the radio. After I radioed the coast guard, all we could do was sit tight and wait. I joined Marcia in the cabin below. She was sobbing by now and saying, 'Hank, I'm so scared.' I sat next to her and held her tightly in my arms. I think I was more scared than she was, but thankfully we heard the coast guard siren before we could come to harm and were led to safety.

"Every now and then, I think of that hug. I'm convinced it was the anchor that got us through the whole ordeal."

One of Laura's favorite memories is one of hugging her husband when she won a four-day trip to the Bahamas. Laura was an account representative for a trucking company and was attending an annual sales dinner. "One of the other account reps talked me into entering the drawing. I had never won anything in my life, but I figured I couldn't win if I didn't enter, so I bought some raffle tickets. I couldn't believe it when my number was drawn. When I went up to the podium and accepted the prize, the only thing I could say was, 'I can't wait to tell my husband.'

"All the way home, I fantasized about how to tell him. I decided I would sneak into the house, put on my bikini, and prance around until he asked me what

in the world I was doing. My plans never material-
ized. I was so excited that the minute I walked into
the house, I spilled the beans. I ran to him screaming,
'We won, we won!' and jumped into his arms, wrap-
ping my legs around his waist. When I showed him
the prize, Ray swung me around and around as we
hugged each other tightly. It was a hug I'll never forget!"

There will be times in your relationship when your
mate is crabby, argumentative, unreasonable, and
seems anxious to pick a fight. At times like these, the
last thing you'll want to do is hug him or her.

But guess what? That's the time when your mate
needs a hug the most. There's nothing like a warm
embrace to calm and soothe a cantankerous partner.

Esther told me how this had been exactly what her
husband, Chuck, had needed the Saturday before our
conversation. It was hot and humid and Chuck had
been working in the yard since early morning. Nothing was going right. The lawn mower wouldn't start,
the weed eater broke, and a shovel that had been
leaning against the garage fell and made a huge dent
in his brand new car.

"When Chuck came in for lunch, he was really a
bear," said Esther. "When I tried to talk to him, he
growled at me. I could hear how tense he was by the
sound of his breathing. He was doing a lot of huffing
and puffing. When he started blaming me for hiding
his sunglasses, I knew what he needed. I went over to
him and gave him a nice, long bear hug. As I held
him, I could feel his muscles relax and his breathing
slow down. We hugged until I heard him say,
'Thanks, I needed that.' "

What About Me?

On any given day, there is at least one reason to hug your mate. But what if you want a hug? If your mate isn't forthcoming with hugs, then ask for one. If you went through your day and wrote down every time you wanted a hug, you'd probably have a list that looks like this:

15 Reasons to Ask Your Mate for a Hug
1. You're tired.
2. You're scared.
3. You're turned on.
4. You're cold.
5. You're stressed.
6. You've just come home.
7. You're leaving.
8. You're going to bed.
9. You've just awakened.
10. You're proud of yourself.
11. You're in emotional pain.
12. You're in physical pain.
13. You're sick.
14. You feel playful.
15. For no reason at all.

While working in her rose garden recently, Theresa had an opportunity to ask her husband, Mike, for a hug. One morning she was busy doing what she loved to do most: pruning, replanting, and weeding, while Mike read the newspaper on their patio. Although she was wearing gardening gloves, a rose thorn punctured the skin in her thumb.

"I must have grabbed the stem pretty hard for the thorn to penetrate the glove and my thumb," said Theresa. "I got it out, but my thumb bled for quite a while. It really hurt!"

After Theresa pulled the thorn out and wiped a tear from her eye, she went over to show Mike her wound. "I remember feeling like a little girl," said Theresa. "After my husband agreed that what I did must have really hurt, I looked at him forlornly and said, 'Can I have a hug?'

"He said, 'Sure' and opened his arms. I sat on his lap and put my head on his shoulder as he gave me a strong, loving hug. It made me feel a lot better."

Instead of asking to be hugged for cuts and bruises, my daughter Tara and her husband, Mark, have learned how to turn tension into tenderness. Whenever they face a stressful situation, one of them will turn to the other and say, "Hug break!" They agreed a long time ago that no matter how stressed they are, if one of them asks for a "hug break," the other will comply.

They used this technique while planning their wedding, buying their first home, and purchasing furniture. "It worked every time," said Tara. "Our hug breaks would relieve the stress and give us the energy we needed to keep going."

Although not used to asking for what he wants in a relationship, Carl admitted to asking for a hug from his girlfriend, Sharon.

"I travel a lot in my business," said Carl. "In the four years that Sharon and I have been dating, it feels like I've gone around the world at least twice. My traveling is so routine that my leave-taking had become routine too. Sharon would drive me to the airport, give me a quick kiss on the lips, and wave as she pulled her car away from the curb. Once I was seated on the plane, I felt like I was missing something. What I was missing was a good-bye connection with Sharon. So when she drove me to the airport the next time and leaned over to give me one of those quick kisses, I covered her mouth with my hand and authoritatively said, 'Sharon, get out of the car.' She looked at me like I was crazy, but she got out.

"We stood there with the trunk of the car open, the motor running, and the skycap waiting impatiently, as I said, 'How about a hug?' Sharon looked a bit surprised, but laughed and said, 'Sure thing.' We stood there hugging for at least a minute. I didn't need to get on a plane to feel like I was flying that day!"

When a Hug Is Not a Hug

Just as some hugs are more significant than others, some are more satisfying than others. Many people in the seminars I teach say they would like to hug more if their loved one just wouldn't pat them or rub them on the back in the process.

As I covered this topic in class one night, Louise suddenly spoke up as if a light bulb had gone off in her head. "That's it!"

When I asked her, "What's it?" she replied, "That's why I never feel a connection with my husband when he hugs me. He does that patting thing." Louise went on to explain how insincere the hug felt when her husband patted her on the back as if she were a child. She said it felt like he was patronizing her and saying, "Now, now, baby, it's all right."

When she broached the subject with Don, he said he didn't intend for his hug to feel condescending at all. He admitted that he could see why she would think of it that way, though. Now when they embrace, Don encircles Louise in his arms and holds her lovingly to him.

In a similar vein, Joe explained in the men's class one night how his girlfriend, Samantha, hugged him. "I don't know if she has nervous energy or what, but when we hug, she keeps rubbing her hand up and down on my back. The next thing I know, it feels like she's burping me. I really don't like it at all."

I suggested to Joe that he talk with Samantha about it. He did, using the four-step formula he had learned in class the week before. What he learned was that Samantha's parents had always hugged her that way. She had never really experienced the intensity of a warm, long-lasting hug. After Joe taught Samantha how to hug without rubbing his back she was able to receive the hug, as well as give it. She really enjoyed the difference.

The K.I.S.S. Plan

After reading this chapter, I'm sure you'll agree that touch is one of the most important human needs there is. It's obvious that it's at least as important as nourishment and rest, because without it infants die. And without touch, your relationship will also die.

Keep your relationship alive and **Keep It Something Special** by making touch a staple in your life together.

Starting today, I want you to touch your mate at least once a day. It doesn't matter whether you rub, tickle, scratch, massage, or caress your mate. What matters is that you touch each other every day.

I want one of the ways you touch during the week to be a twenty-second hug—not two seconds, not five seconds, not fifteen seconds—but a full twenty seconds! Timing is critical here. It takes at least five seconds to block out all the outside distractions and focus in on your mate. Once you've done that, it takes an additional fifteen seconds to stay in the present moment with your mate as you exchange loving energy.

When hugging, it is important to remember that not only are you giving, you are receiving. Just as with the ten-second kiss, when you engage in a twenty-second hug, you and your mate begin to breathe in unison with each other. You infuse each other with your life force as you become one. If you are concentrating only on giving, this sacred exchange of energy cannot take place.

When giving a hug, focus on sending love from your heart. When receiving a hug, focus on taking love in through your heart. If you take the time to feel both the giving and the receiving, your hug will nurture you, your mate, and your relationship.

5

THE
SIXTY-MINUTE
SEDUCTION

A Loving Connection

You can pick them out in a crowd. They have energy and zip—a little extra bounce in their step. They touch frequently, exchange loving looks, laugh at each other's jokes. Who are they? A couple with a good sex life, of course.

Partners who are used to sharing their sexuality are easy to spot and enjoyable to watch. My husband and I recently met such a couple at a retreat where we had gone for a week of rest and relaxation. Living proof that sexuality does not diminish with age, Ruth and Perry were both in their seventies and had been married for over fifty years.

Two years ago Ruth discovered a large tumor behind her right knee. It was malignant, and Ruth required surgery and chemotherapy. Because of the size and location of the tumor, there was considerable concern about whether Ruth would be able to walk again after the surgery. Perry, who told us he felt lucky to be in good health and able to give her the care she needed, became Ruth's caretaker for the next several months. Ruth told us proudly that she attributed her recovery and her ability to walk again to the tender loving care her husband had given her.

Perry and Ruth confided that they had always had a close, loving relationship, but this scare had made them both realize how little time they might have left. They were determined not to waste a single minute.

My husband and I could not help but notice how playful and romantic they were together and how attentive they were to each other's needs. They held hands everywhere they went. Perry was very protective of Ruth, who still walked with a slight limp. He was quick to hold doors open for her and pull her chair out before they sat down to meals. Ruth was always very interested in what Perry was ordering to eat, making sure that the food was just the way he wanted it. When dessert came, they tasted each other's choices, feeding each other from their own plates. It was a pleasure to see how much they enjoyed each other's company.

They were also very active and enjoyed attending parties and dances together. As it happened, Halloween fell during the week of the retreat, and Perry and Ruth were leaving the grounds to go to a friend's party. Decked out as pirates, they came into the dining room to show everyone their costumes. As they started to leave, Perry winked and said, "I'll get my real treasure when we get home later tonight." Ruth laughed and said, "Only if you're a good buccaneer."

One time, we noticed them slow dancing together. They seemed oblivious to their surroundings, whispering into each other's ears and smiling or chuckling at something the other had said. Another time, Ruth sat on Perry's lap during a lecture because the chair was too hard and he wanted her to be more comfortable.

There was no doubt in our minds that this couple still enjoyed an active sex life. These two people, who had remained lovers for over fifty years, were an inspiration to all of us. The sparkle in their eyes will remain in our memories for a very long time as proof of the power that the sexual connection has in a relationship.

Sixty Minutes of Love

There are many kinds of sexual connection possible between mates. There's the passionate, purely physical release of sexual connection. There's the highly erotic quickie. There's the kind of sex performed out of a sense of duty, and there's the sexual connection everybody wants, but seldom gets—the sixty-minute seduction.

This is the kind of sex you plan for, anticipate, prepare for. You linger over it, and after it's over you savor it for hours, days, or weeks. The sixty-minute seduction is an opportunity for you to let your partner know how much they are loved by giving them pleasure and letting them pleasure you in all the ways you desire.

Couples who connect daily with a hug, a kiss, and

deep communication will naturally want to continue this level of intimacy in the bedroom. Just as the body, mind, and spirit cannot be separated, all the aspects of your relationship are interconnected. Caring and kindness outside of the bedroom will be a part of your sexual relationship. Couples who have fun and are playful in their daily life will be playful in bed as well. Couples who practice communication skills routinely will communicate well in the bedroom. And just as the body requires food and water to remain healthy, your relationship requires regular sexual intimacy for optimal health.

The Sexual Road to Health

We are sexual beings, and an active, satisfying sex life is an important factor in our overall health. When we make love, we breathe more deeply, increasing our intake of oxygen. With more oxygen in our bloodstream, our heart pumps more efficiently, which helps move the oxygen throughout our entire body. Increased circulation adds a healthy glow to our skin, shine to our hair, and a sparkle to our eyes. In addition, sexual arousal and orgasm causes our brain to release chemicals called endorphins, which contain painkilling elements. But the biggest benefit of a healthy sex life may be the effect it has on our immune system. Dr. Paul Pearsall, the director of several sexual-treatment clinics throughout the country, has studied the direct effect of sexual intimacy on people's immune systems. He found that as mates whose sexual connection was infrequent or nonexistent reconnected sexually, they reported fewer and fewer symptoms from headaches, premenstrual syndrome, and arthritis.

There is no question that life outside the bedroom must be nurtured by doing things like talking on a deep level, complimenting, and touching nonsexually. It takes a lot of energy to maintain your relationship, and if it isn't maintained, your lovemaking will be either very shallow or nonexistent. What most people fail to understand is that your relationship "between the sheets" requires a lot of care and attention as well. It has a life of its own and needs just as much nurturing as your relationship outside of the bedroom.

Fizzle Prevention

Most people simply accept the fact that sex with the same partner will become boring and routine over time, but that certainly doesn't have to be the case. You can have hot sex, tender sex, quick sex, or slow sex—you can have sex any way you like it if you and your partner are willing to put some thought and energy into it.

How would you rate your sex life at this moment? Does it still have the sizzle that characterized it early in your relationship or, like last night's champagne, has it begun to fizzle and go flat? To find out how much sizzle is left in your sex life, take the "Fizz Quiz" below.

Sexual Fizz Quiz

- Do you enjoy making love to your mate?
- Do you let your mate know how much you desire him or her?
- Do you carve out special time for lovemaking?
- Do you create a romantic atmosphere that is conducive to making love?
- Do you tell your mate what feels good during lovemaking?
- Do you compliment your mate on his or her body before, during, or after lovemaking?
- While making love, are you as comfortable with the lights on as you are with them off?
- Do you vary the time of day you make love?
- Do you try different positions when making love?
- Do you allow sufficient time for foreplay before making love?

If you answered "no" to more than half of the questions, my guess is that your sex life has begun to fizzle. Read on to see how you can brighten up a dull sex life with a few simple steps. Before you know it, the bubbles will be back and your relationship will sparkle again.

To Turn It Around, Look Around

If your sex life with your mate has lost its sparkle, an obvious place to begin to revive it is in the bedroom. When was the last time you looked at your bedroom as a romantic hideaway, rather than a place to crash at the end of the day? If your bedroom resembles a crash pad more than a boudoir, it's probably time to do what Jacqueline did. As unbelievable as it may sound, Jacqueline's catalyst for improving her sexual relationship with her husband was a serious bout of flu that kept her bedridden for a week.

"I remember lying in bed day after day, feeling miserable," said Jacqueline. "I don't know what made me feel worse, the flu or staring at a dark, dismal, laundry-infested bedroom all week."

"For seven long days, I watched as our bedroom was used as a home office, a storage area for Barbie dolls and Legos, and a dumping ground for dirty clothes. After the third day of tripping over a laundry basket every time I went to the bathroom, I vowed I was going to make our bedroom into the love nest it was meant to be.

"As soon as I had the energy, I began the makeover. Thanks to the *Light His Fire* tapes, I knew exactly what to do. I started with our bed linens, replacing the low-thread-count polyesters with beautiful satin sheets. Then I replaced the boring white light bulbs with red ones. I placed scented candles around the room to get rid of the smell of dirty laundry. And I bought some romantic CDs to play on our CD player, which I had hidden under a table.

"When my husband saw our transformed bedroom for the very first time, he beamed. That night he told me he had begun to worry that our relationship was taking on the same aura as our bedroom—dull and dingy. Now that our bedroom has brightened up, so has our sex life."

Jacqueline and her husband learned how important it was to pay attention to their bedroom. Your bedroom reflects the pulse of your sex life. In Carter and Jacqueline's case, their pulse was weak and irregular.

We spend more time in our bedroom than we do in any other room of our home. It should be a private sanctuary where you and your mate can be alone together, away from the pressures and distractions of the outside world. A bedroom makeover doesn't require a degree in interior design or a lot of money. All you need is the desire to create a private haven where you and your mate can share your sexuality in the safety of each other's arms.

Carve Out Time

Even after you've transformed your bedroom into a romantic retreat, don't be surprised if the demands of daily life interfere with your ability to spend time in the love nest you've created.

That's why I tell couples to schedule sex on their calendars. As rigid as that might sound, it's the best way to ensure that you and your mate stay sexually connected. Our lives have become so complicated that today even schoolchildren are required to keep an appointment organizer noting homework assignments, social engagements, extracurricular activities, dental appointments, music lessons, and other dates. As parents, your calendar includes your children's schedules, as well as your own. With such a hectic life, it's easy to let your sex life take a back seat to your other commitments. But the most important commitment in your life is the one you made to your partner. Instead of waiting to make love until the time is right, you must create the time by planning it in advance.

Bernadine, a woman in one of my *Light His Fire* classes, told me how surprised she was when she learned her sister scheduled sex with her husband.

"I can't believe it," Bernadine said. "My little sister puts stickers on her calendar to remind herself and her husband to have sex! Can't they remember?"

Bernadine went on to explain that her sister is a waitress and her brother-in-law is a musician. Between long restaurant hours and late-night gigs, they often go for days without connecting.

I told Bernadine that her sister was a very wise woman. She already knew one of the keys to a healthy sex life . . . putting sex on her calendar. And why not? We put everything else on our calendars, from dental appointments to car checkups. Our sex life with our partner should certainly be given the same priority.

Scheduling time for sex is a little like putting money aside for the future. If you save money on a regular basis, you will always have a nest egg to rely on if times get rough. By scheduling sex on a regular basis, you will always have an intimate connection with your mate to fall back on in times of stress.

In addition, people who plan for sex relish the anticipation they experience from knowing ahead of time that they are going to make love. A man who has sex scheduled on his calendar is more likely to be sensual and sensitive, instead of using sex as a way of simply relieving sexual tension. A woman who has sex scheduled on her calendar is more likely to be eager for sex, having had ample time to prepare herself both mentally and physically.

Anyone who is familiar with my philosophy knows that I have a formula for long-range planning as well. So that couples can enjoy the feeling of anticipating being together, I suggest the following:

- Every couple should have a date night once a week—a time when they go out alone together, without the distraction of their children, friends, or business associates.
- Every three months, a couple needs to go away overnight—again, just the two of them.
- Once each year, couples should get away alone together for an entire week.

By setting aside time to concentrate exclusively on each other, a couple can feel secure in the knowledge that they will have an intimate and deep relationship with each other for the rest of their lives.

Tonight's the Night

There are lots of ways to plan ahead and let your mate know you are interested in sharing some intimate time together. Here are some playful ways to let your mate know that you desire him or her sexually:

- When scheduling sex on your calendar, use a pen with different colored ink for the days you want to make love.
- Have a decorative pillow on your bed with two

different designs on either side. Agree to leave a particular side of the pillow showing on the days you want to make love.

- Leave a note in your mate's lunch, briefcase, or purse.
- Have a special magnet you put on your refrigerator for the days you want to make love.
- Call your mate and ring only once, then hang up.
- Wrap a rubber band around you mate's toothbrush to tell him or her that today is the day!
- Put a candy heart in your mate's shoe as a reminder.
- Replace the white light bulb in your bedroom lamp with a red one when you are ready for some lovemaking.
- Put a smiley-face sticker on the steering wheel of your mate's car.

Clear Your Calendar and Your Mind

What happens if your mate has let you know that he or she is in the mood for love, but making love is the last thing on your mind? Instead of rejecting your mate's impulse to connect with you, or agreeing reluctantly to making love, get into a lovemaking frame of mind.

Please don't misunderstand. There are certainly times when it is perfectly acceptable to say no to lovemaking. No one should feel duty-bound to have sex if they don't want to. But when you and your mate are just on different wavelengths, when you feel like tuning out instead of turning on, your sexuality is simply a question of mind over matter. It's commonly accepted that your mind is your most erogenous zone, so change your mind and the feelings will follow.

Being tired is as much a psychological state as a physical one. For example, you may feel totally exhausted at the end of a long day, with no other thought than to fall into bed as soon as possible. But if Ed McMahon were to ring your doorbell and say you had just won the Publishers Clearing House Sweepstakes, you would suddenly have more energy than you'd know what to do with. Your desire to fall into bed would be replaced by exuberance as your mind overflowed with thoughts of how you'd use the money. Just as a change of mind can energize you, a change of mind can signal your body to be responsive to the idea of lovemaking.

If your mate has given you a sign, most likely he or she has done it in advance, allowing you an excellent opportunity to prepare yourself for lovemaking.

I know of one particular couple who have a wonderful sexual relationship. When I asked Lynne her secret, she told me she makes it a practice to be available to her husband whenever he expresses a desire to make love, even though she is seldom in the mood when he is. "I just get myself into a lovemaking frame of mind," she said.

I asked her to explain.

"Well, for example, one day last week my husband left a note in my purse telling me how much he was looking forward to our kids going to bed that night, so that we could have some private time together.

"I have to admit that when I saw the note, the idea

of making love left me cold. I had a particularly busy day at the office and I still had a long list of things to do for that evening," said Lynne. "The last thing on my mind was making love. But, rather than closing my mind to Aaron's sexual advance, I asked him to help me with some of my chores. He agreed to make some phone calls for me and to get the kids ready for bed, while I took the time to wind down.

"I retreated to the bathroom, where I prepared a nice, warm bubble bath, lit a candle, and played some calming music on the radio. As I lay in the tub, I began to clear my mind of all the day's business. I let myself think of absolutely nothing except how good it felt to soak in a warm tub. Gradually, I began to let sexual thoughts creep into my consciousness. Mentally, I replayed one of my favorite memories of Aaron and me making love. As I watched the scene unfold in my mind, I could feel sexual feelings begin to stir.

"I left nothing out of my sensual daydream, from how we undressed each other down to the sound of our lustful breathing. I let myself remember every passionate detail. By the time I drained the tub and toweled myself dry, I was relaxed and eager to join my husband in bed."

Even though it's a generally accepted notion that men are always ready to make love, I believe there has been a change in recent years. Men and women today are under incredible pressure to perform in their jobs, fulfill family responsibilities, spend time keeping fit, and maintain an active social life. In addition, a man is expected to be a good lover, attentive to his wife's needs as well as his own. With all this pressure, it is not unusual for a man to have difficulty getting into a lovemaking mind-set. I remember one particular student who worked very hard. After listening to my tapes, Clarence became aware that his habit of working long into the night was a self-imposed hardship—one he could control. Late one night as Clarence sat at his computer preparing a business presentation, his wife began rubbing his neck and shoulders.

"Charisse's touch felt so good. I had been working in the same position for almost two hours," said Clarence. "When she suggested I stop for the night and join her in bed, I told her I'd be down in a little while.

"After she left the room, I found myself getting back into my work, but when I smelled Charisse's perfume and heard her playing soft music in the bedroom I turned off my computer immediately. But I knew I had to turn off the work-related chatter in my mind as well. Before joining Charisse, I took a few deep breaths and imagined the passionate lovemaking we were about to share. Within minutes my mind was ready. Within seconds, my body followed."

Like Lynne and Clarence, you can open yourself to your sexuality, even when you aren't feeling sexual. Your relationship with your mate depends on seizing the opportunities for sex when your partner expresses an interest, rather than waiting for the time when you are in the mood, too. Follow these steps to get yourself into a lovemaking frame of mind:

- Put yourself in a relaxing environment with no distractions.

- Take time to clear your mind of unwanted thoughts and replace them with sexual thoughts.
- Use all of your senses to imagine a sensual encounter between yourself and your mate. Let yourself hear, see, smell, feel, and even taste the passion!

Your Mate Is Worth the Trouble

Scheduling sex not only offers you an opportunity to prepare your mind for your sensual time with your mate, but gives you a chance to prepare yourself physically as well. Taking the time and trouble for personal hygiene and making yourself attractive lets your mate know he or she matters to you.

For example, Clay, a student in one of my men's classes, was an auto mechanic. Although he showered every night before going to bed, his wife complained about the dirt and grease under his fingernails and the roughness of his hands. After learning of his wife's distaste, Clay began using a nailbrush to clean his nails and lotion to keep his hands soft. "Now Amelia goes on and on about my clean hands and soft skin. I guess my keeping my nails clean and my hands soft makes her feel she's important to me," Clay said.

If your mate's personal hygiene habits are a turn-off to you, use your thirty-minute talk time to approach the subject. Let your mate know, in a loving way, that you would respond favorably to a change in that area. Francine told me it had never occurred to her that what she wore to bed was important to her husband until he mentioned it to her one night. "I'm always cold," Francine told me. "To me, perfect bedtime attire is either a flannel nightgown or long underwear and socks.

"One evening, Lyle and I had a talk about my bedtime wardrobe. He told me that when he sees me leave the house for work every day looking good enough to eat, and then sees me come to bed looking like Nanook of the North, he feels like he doesn't matter to me.

"If we hadn't talked about it, I never would have known he felt that way. After our talk, I started giving my bedtime wardrobe as much thought as I give my business wardrobe. In fact, I take Lyle shopping with me and with his help I have acquired a wonderful collection of lingerie. Now, instead of putting on my long johns, I cuddle up to Lyle to keep warm."

The Pressure Is Off

Although it's important to stay sexually connected to your mate and to plan for sex in the same way that you plan for the other activities of your life together, there is no need to feel pressured to have sex on any particular time schedule. There are no rules about how often a couple should have sex. The only people who matter are you and your mate.

Unfortunately, many people are competitive about sex. They want to be sure they are having sex as often, if not more often, than everyone else. We're a nation driven by competition and a desire to keep up with the Joneses. When it comes to sex, that competition turns into a numbers game. I'm always being asked how many times per week a couple should have sex. While regular sex is good for you and good for your relationship, how often you and your mate make love depends entirely on what is mutually agreeable for you. For some people, regular means every day, for others it means every week, and for still others it means every two weeks. There is no right or wrong here. The key is that you both feel fulfilled and connected sexually, as well as spiritually and emotionally.

People who keep a sexual scorecard end up like a man in one of my classes who traded sexual enjoyment for sexual performance. Tim jumped at every opportunity to tell the other men in class how active his sex life with his wife was, even bragging that one of the proudest moments of his life was when he was able to have sex after having had a vasectomy the same day.

People pressure themselves over many things: making more money, getting a better job, collecting more possessions, or becoming more popular. But pressuring yourself about how often to have sex will only lead to anxiety and tension. Make love because it's right for you and your mate—not because it's time to satisfy some imaginary statistic.

The Best Aphrodisiac

When it comes to aphrodisiacs, the right words spoken at the right time are a powerful turn-on. Talking to each other while making love, whether in whispers or tribal calls, can enrich your sex life dramatically.

One woman who took my *Light His Fire* class said that her husband actually talks to her more when they make love than at other times during the day. "He's a man of few words outside of the bedroom, but get him between the sheets and he turns into a real talker. I love it when he talks to me, because I know he's in the present moment with me rather than thinking of a million other things."

Cassie, another woman in my class, shared that she and her husband sometimes read to each other before making love. "There is a lot of erotic literature available," she said. "My husband and I take turns reading. It's a wonderful method of foreplay. For us, hearing each other's voices is much more exciting than watching an erotic video."

Lovemaking is a perfect time to shower your mate with compliments. Think about it. There you are, in each other's arms, with an excellent opportunity to touch and admire each other's bodies in a way you can't possibly do when fully clothed.

Immerse yourself in your mate's essence, using all of your senses. Enjoy the feel of her soft curves or his hard muscles. Savor the scent of your mate's body or the fragrance of a favorite perfume or cologne. Delight in your partner's body as you watch him or her move during lovemaking. But whatever you do, don't keep your pleasure to yourself. Share it with your mate. Tell your mate how exciting he or she is, how much you enjoy the way he or she looks, tastes, feels, and smells.

Talking while making love is a way to relish each

other during your sexual union. But for women, especially, talking immediately after lovemaking is just as meaningful. It's as important to most women to hear words of love after sex as it is before and during lovemaking. Many women have told me that they feel closer to their mates after they make love than they do at any other time, allowing them to share intimate thoughts and feelings that are normally difficult to share.

What's Your Pleasure?

Talking during lovemaking is the best way I know of to avoid getting caught in the trap of mind reading. The blissful euphoria of sexual union can easily turn into a case of silent guesswork if neither partner tells the other what makes him or her feel good.

You're at the helm. Your mission is to direct, guide, and navigate so your partner knows exactly what direction to take to satisfy you. The best way to get more of what you already enjoy is to tell your partner how good it feels. Phrases like "That's it," "Right there," "That's good," and "Keep going" are simple but direct messages to encourage your mate to continue what he or she is doing. Your talent as a sexual director is limited only by your imagination. You can describe your pleasure with adjectives, analogies, or one-word exclamations.

A woman in one of my classes told us she knows exactly when she's done a good job of sexually satisfying her husband. "He's good at letting me know what he likes, but when he starts talking in Japanese, I know I've hit the jackpot," she said.

No matter how you choose to direct your mate, the important thing to remember is that he or she cannot read your mind, or sometimes even your body language. Often during orgasm, it's hard to tell whether a facial expression reflects pleasure or pain—one more reason why it's necessary to tell your mate what feels good. It's equally important to tell your mate if something he or she is doing doesn't feel good. The best way to do this is to redirect your mate. After telling your partner what is uncomfortable, suggest another way that he or she can please you. Expressing only your discomfort, without telling your mate what would feel good, may discourage your partner from trying to please you at all.

Jack, a man in my *Light Her Fire* class, told us he made a few mistakes before he learned how to ask his wife for what felt good to him. "I really blew it," said Jack. "I'm so used to bossing people around on the job, that I think I ended up doing that in bed with my wife. I didn't realize it at the time, but when we made love, I would only tell her when she was doing something that didn't feel good. I would actually bark at her and say, 'Not like that,' or 'That's too hard.' One time she got so frustrated, she said, 'Just do it yourself then,' and left the bedroom."

Since taking the class, Jack has learned the art of sexual redirection. Instead of telling his wife only what doesn't feel good, he now lets her know what she can do differently to please him. Rather than barking orders at her, Jack has learned to gently tell his wife when her touch feels uncomfortable. When she touches him in the way he suggests, Jack reinforces her newfound touch by saying, "That's great, honey. I love it when you do that."

Most people are timid at first about giving their mate direction in bed, but if you've been doing your K.I.S.S. Plan at the end of each chapter, this shouldn't be difficult. Be sensitive to your mate's feelings, being careful not to offend him or her. Timing is important, and if this will be a big change, you may want to discuss it with your partner before beginning to express yourself in the bedroom. Once you and your mate get used to telling each other what you like and dislike, you'll soon feel comfortable exploring new areas of intimacy. When you show your partner that you have a track record of listening to and following his or her directions, look out! You never know in which direction you'll be led next.

Setting the Scene

Even the most open, honest, and communicative lovemaking can become boring after a while. Talking to your mate while making love is wonderful, but if you say the same things, at the same times, in the same place, every time you make love, your sex life can go flat.

Many couples use sexual fantasy to enhance their sex life. By using your imagination to create a sexual scenario, you can vary your lovemaking routine and put some sparkle back in your relationship. Your description can be as graphic and detailed as you want it to be. Although this may feel a little awkward at first, you're the storyteller, so have fun painting a picture for your partner.

Once you have a sexual scenario in mind, approach your mate by saying, "Let's pretend . . ." As you begin to relate a story to your mate, remember that you are in the safety of your lover's arms. Just relax and follow your imagination wherever it takes you.

During my years of teaching, certain couples have felt comfortable enough to share some of their sexual scenarios with me. One husband told me he painted a scene for his wife by saying, "Let's pretend we don't know each other and we're in a grocery store. As we're both looking for something in the same aisle, we end up banging into each other's grocery carts. The food in my cart tumbles to the floor. You apologize for bumping into my cart, and bend over to help me pick up my groceries. As I watch you pick up the food, I am mesmerized by your beauty. I am particularly attracted to your classic facial features: your high cheekbones, your gorgeous wide-set eyes, and your full sensuous lips."

The husband said he felt a little uncomfortable at first, but the more he followed his imagination, the more he relaxed. Once he felt his wife respond with warmth and appreciation, their lovemaking changed from routine to lively.

Stacey, a woman I met at one of my lectures, told me of a sexual fantasy she presents to her husband now and then while making love. As they lie in each other's arms, her story begins with, "Let's pretend we've never met and are both driving on the freeway, when suddenly I get a flat tire. I pull over to the side of the road and put on my hazard lights in hopes that someone will stop to help me. You see me in distress and pull off the road behind my car. I explain to you that I have a spare and some tools, but I have no idea how to change a tire. You tell me not to worry and that you'll have my spare tire on in no time. It's a hot day, so you take off your shirt to begin working on my car. You instruct me step-by-step how to change a tire, but I can't concentrate on what you're saying because I'm distracted by your fabulous body. I can't help but stare at your bulging biceps and your strong, wide shoulders. I want so much to reach out and touch you, but I know I can't. Before long, my tire is fixed, and your shirt is back on. I reach out to shake your hand, and . . .

Stacey told me that this scenario is her husband's favorite. Each time she tells it, she admires and longs for different parts of his body. He says that by the end of her story he feels like Rambo.

One couple told me that they like to make up a sexual scenario together. "One of us will start the story and the other is allowed to add to it at any time. Neither of us knows exactly how the story will turn out. We find it exciting."

Many couples have told me that inventing stories during lovemaking adds a hot combination of spontaneity, sexuality, and imagination to their relationship. If you'd like to experience the fun of a sexual scenario, but feel your imagination needs a boost, scan the list below for ideas.

School Days

You and your mate meet each other for the first time while taking a night class at a local college. You discover you live in the same neighborhood and decide to study together. Why is it you're having trouble concentrating?

It All Adds Up

You're an accountant, and you've just started a job at an accounting firm. The first day on the job, you meet your mate. You are both assigned to work together on a tax return for the company's biggest client. As you work together, side by side, you concentrate on each other's figures more than the figures on the spreadsheet.

If the Shoe Fits

You go shopping one afternoon for a pair of shoes. As you peruse the selection of footwear, your mate, who is the salesperson, asks if you need any help. You are struck by how attractive your mate is and tell him or her that you would like to try on some shoes. Before your shopping spree is over, you decide to handle your mate rather than just the merchandise.

Order in the Court

You meet your mate while you're both serving jury duty on the same trial. You have a problem understanding the details of the case because you'd rather sentence your mate . . . to a night of mad, passionate lovemaking with you.

On Your Mark, Get Set, Go!

You are registered to run in a marathon. This is your first time running in a competition. To keep from dropping too far behind, you set your sights on the gorgeous creature in front of you—your mate. You enjoy watching every muscle in his or her body work as you race to the finish.

Worth the Wait

While alone at an amusement park one day, you wait in line for two hours to get on a roller coaster. As you step into the roller coaster car, you see that you are sharing it with an exceptionally attractive person—your mate. As the ride attendant tightens the safety belt across both of your laps, you get ready for a bigger thrill than you had expected.

Special Delivery

You are a U.P.S. deliveryperson, and you have a special delivery for your mate. You ring the doorbell. When your mate answers, you ask him or her to sign for the delivery. While waiting for the signature, you give your mate a list of reasons why he or she should invite you in.

Checkmate

You and your mate are in a chess tournament. Your mate is so desirable that you are having great difficulty planning your strategy. To distract your mate, you tell him or her about all of the moves you're going to make. Not in the game, but on your mate!

Playing Taps

You and your mate meet for the first time while taking a tap dance class together. During class, you can't help but stare at your mate's body as he or she shuffle-ball-changes. During a break, you tell your mate how you'd like to tap into him or her.

Once you get comfortable using sexual scenarios in your lovemaking, you will have created a romantic, sensual, and passionate world for you and your mate, a world without boundaries!

The K.I.S.S. Plan

Your sexual union with your partner is a precious gift. **K**eep **I**t **S**omething **S**pecial by giving it the loving energy it deserves.

Pay attention to the atmosphere you've created in your bedroom. Making love in a room that you and your mate have worked at to make romantic and sensual will be a constant reminder to keep your sexuality a top priority.

Learn to talk to each other during lovemaking. Compliment your mate on his or her body and sensuality. A running commentary isn't necessary, but loving positive feedback is something we all long for.

Tell your partner what pleases you. He or she can't read your mind. Ask your mate what it is that pleases him or her. Listen to your mate's likes and dislikes so that you'll know which direction to take.

Carve out time for your sexuality, even if it means scheduling sex on your calendar. Watch for those secret messages from your mate telling you that he or she wants to make love to you.

Practice getting into a lovemaking mind-set. Remember, even if you are somewhat tired, your body will follow the direction your mind gives it. Training yourself to feel more sexual will enhance and deepen your intimacy with your mate.

Prepare yourself not only mentally but physically before making love to your mate. Making the effort to keep yourself clean and attractive for lovemaking shows your partner how much he or she matters to you.

6

THE
TWO-HOUR
FANTASY

Dare to Dream

*W*hen I get to the topic of fantasy in my classes, I often get mixed reactions. Some people's faces light up with a grin. Others remain very quiet and don't crack a smile. Still others look a little puzzled. One of them might say, "But I don't fantasize."

"Yes, you do," I retort.

Everybody fantasizes. If people didn't fantasize, Disneyland wouldn't exist. A fantasy is nothing more than a dream. It can be a dream you hope one day to realize, or it can be a dream that is so private you wouldn't share it with anyone but your mate. I'll bet you and your mate have shared lots of dreams and fantasies over the years. Just think about how many times you've heard your mate say, "I wish . . ."

Well, how would you like to make your mate's dreams come true?

Believe it or not, it is within your power to grant your mate's wishes, and I'm going to show you how. All it takes is the desire to please your partner, along with some time and effort, a little imagination, and some help from me. By the end of this chapter you will have all the tools you need to produce a fantasy for your mate that will blow his or her socks off.

Does your mate dream about being treated like a princess? It is within your power to make her queen for a day. Does he dream about being a test pilot? You can put him at the controls for an evening of flying high. Maybe her dream is to be a big winner at the Academy Awards. You can give her an Oscar all her own. Does your mate dream about being forced to submit to your sexual allure? Piece of cake!

A fantasy doesn't have to be bigger than life to be worthy of attention. Many women dream of being surprised with breakfast in bed. One man I know told me his fantasy was to spend an entire day in his pajamas and to nap anytime he wanted to. These are dreams that you can make come true. I'm not pretending that creating a fantasy for your loved one will always be easy. It may take a tremendous amount of effort. There will likely be a great deal of advance planning required, costumes and props to be gathered; you may even need to solicit the cooperation of others in order to make your mate's fantasy a reality. But the energy you spend bringing your mate's fantasy to life will fuel your relationship and keep it hot for the months to come.

His and Hers

The fantasy you create for your mate might be very different from the one you would create for yourself. Yours might include a secluded spot at the beach or a candlelit table in an intimate restaurant. Your mate's fantasy may be in the shower, in the woods, or in a motel room. Your idea of looking sexy might include velvet and lace, while your mate may find leather and silk a turn-on.

In general, a woman's fantasy satisfies her emotional need to be treasured and adored. Her idea of physical contact, although leading up to making love, would no doubt include a lot of hand-holding, cuddling, and caressing. When I speak to men about creating a woman's fantasy, I have to remind them that the way to a woman's heart is not a beeline to her breasts or genitals. If you are in the habit of taking the initiative sexually in your relationship and your mate tends to feel pressured about making love most of the time, create a romantic, playful, or loving fantasy with no sex involved. Of course, if during the course of the fantasy your mate insists, well . . . who are you to deprive her?

In general, a man's fantasy addresses his need to be loved sexually in as many ways as possible. When I teach women how to create a fantasy for a man, I have to remind them that the way to a man's heart is *not* through his stomach! In fact, the person who came up with that saying was probably a woman who hated sex! Can you imagine a man coming home one day after thirty-five years of marriage and telling his wife, ''I know I've been faithful to you all these years, but I'm leaving you. I've met another woman who makes a pot roast I can't resist"?

I'm not saying that some men may not fantasize about a romantic dinner for two on a tropical beach or that some women may not fantasize about which sex toy to use with their mate. But in my years of teaching men and women how to create fantasies for each other, most men have told me their fantasies revolve around feeling sexually satisfied, and most women have told me their fantasies revolve around feeling emotionally satisfied.

So how do you get your needs met when your mate's needs are the opposite of yours? First of all, you understand that your needs and your mate's needs are not right or wrong—they are simply different. Secondly, you understand you have a choice. You can sit around and wait for your mate to be the first to make the move to create your fantasy and satisfy your needs, or you can forget about who makes the first move and do it yourself.

Over the years I've seen more relationships fail because both partners stubbornly refused to make the first move. I can't stress enough that it makes no difference who does what, when, or how often. All that matters is the result. If you want a relationship that is deep and filled with love, you must be willing to do whatever it takes to make that happen. Yes, it takes effort to keep a relationship special, but it's really unimportant who makes the effort.

A couple in one of my classes experienced the effects of waiting for the other to make the first move, and they weren't happy with the results. This is how they described what happened in their relationship:

"I can feel it when Meg and I are in a downward spiral," said Bob. "There are times when Meg doesn't feel like making love for weeks. During those times, I don't feel like having late-night talks or supporting her in her volunteer work at church."

Meg said, "I hate our stalemate spells. When we haven't had sex for a few weeks, Bob gets irritable and doesn't touch me much or want to share feelings. I know he needs to be sexually intimate, but I get stubborn and refuse because he isn't being supportive."

"Creating fantasies for each other gives us permission to pull out of our downward spiral," said Bob. "Whenever we feel we're in a deadlock, one of us goes to the trouble of setting the scene for a fantasy."

Bob and Meg understood that it didn't matter who was meeting whose needs first. They didn't keep score. What mattered is that one of them, and it didn't matter which one, did something to remind them of their love for each other.

The Payoff

When you create a fantasy for your mate, I want you to do it simply to please and give to your partner. Remember, you're trying to send the message to your mate that he or she is the most important person in your life. Your payoff will be a mate who feels so loved and cared for that he or she will return your love tenfold. We live in a world that operates according to the universal law of cause and effect. What goes around, comes around. As you sow, so shall you reap. If you hold back on your love and support of your mate, that's what you'll get in return—an unloving, unsupportive mate. If, on the other hand, you give love without worrying about what you deserve in return, the love you give your mate will come straight back to you. Your job is to give your love, no matter what form it takes. It can be a compliment, a ten-second kiss, or a fantasy.

He's Leather, She's Lace

Darla and Will's relationship needed a boost. When she stopped to think about it, Darla realized that it had been at least six months since they'd done anything to break their daily routine. They hadn't even had a dinner date alone in all that time. After listening to my *Light His Fire* tapes, Darla decided to create a fantasy for her husband.

She knew that one of Will's fantasies was to visit a local lingerie and sexual paraphernalia store. She had always felt uncomfortable when he brought up the topic of shopping there, and would change the subject to get his mind off it.

"Once I made up my mind to create this fantasy for Will, I was nervous, but I had so much fun planning it," said Darla. "The day I picked him up from work to take him there, I felt like I did the day of our wedding. My heart was pounding so hard I thought it would jump out of my chest, and my palms were so sweaty I could barely grip the steering wheel."

When Will got into the car, Darla blindfolded him

so he wouldn't be able to guess where she was taking him.

"When Darla took off the blindfold and I saw the store, I couldn't believe it," said Will. "I felt like I was in a dream."

Darla and Will walked hand in hand into the store and were faced with counter, wall, and shelf displays of books, games, candles, intimate apparel, and other merchandise that Darla couldn't even identify.

Will let go of Darla's hand and, like a kid in a candy store, headed straight for the sex toys displayed on the back wall. Darla found herself standing frozen next to the display case of chocolate candy in the shape of X-rated body parts. "He owes me bigtime on this one," she thought.

Darla was so uncomfortable that she thought she couldn't stand to be in the store a minute longer. She was about to call to Will that she'd be waiting in the car when she noticed a collection of videos displayed on a shelf. As she reached for one that looked interesting, she bumped a different one, causing a domino effect that brought the entire shelf of X-rated videos crashing around her feet. Just as Darla was calculating how to make her escape, she heard a salesman call to her from across the store, "Do you need some help over there?"

"No, no. No problem. I'm fine," answered Darla, as she scurried to the women's lingerie section.

"I felt more comfortable looking through the lingerie. It almost felt like I was at a regular department store, until Will sauntered up with an outfit he thought I'd look 'dynamite' in," said Darla. "Here I was looking for a feminine, lacy teddy or nightgown I thought would turn Will on, and he shows me this form-fitting leather corset and garter belt combo. I was floored! I never would have thought he'd want me to wear something like that."

As shocked as she was, Darla reminded herself that this was Will's fantasy, not hers. So they bought the outfit, went home, and played out an evening neither of them will ever forget.

Helen, a woman in one of my classes, said that her fantasy was for her husband, Lenny, to whisk her away from her domestic life of carpooling and floor washing and take her on a romantic getaway. Helen's fantasy came true when, for Christmas one year, Lenny sent her on a "love hunt."

The love hunt began when Lenny handed Helen a gift-wrapped videotape. After she opened it, Lenny asked her to slip it into the VCR, and to follow the instructions on the tape.

"I couldn't believe my eyes when I played the video and saw Lenny, standing in a tuxedo, instructing me to go on a love hunt," said Helen.

On the tape, Lenny asked Helen to "pause" the video and look behind the living-room couch. She did, and what she found was another gift. Inside the tiny box was a man's thong bikini swimsuit. Next Helen was to look behind the television set. There she found a bottle of suntan lotion.

"By this time, I was so excited I could barely breathe," said Helen.

Lenny's last instructions were for Helen to look under the front-door mat. When she lifted the doormat, she found two airline tickets to Miami! Thrilled,

Helen threw her arms around Lenny to thank him. "You're not done yet," he said.

Helen turned on the video again to see her husband proudly announcing that he was taking her on a three-day cruise to the Bahamas. "I felt more romanced that night than ever before in our marriage," said Helen. "I was overwhelmed by his thoughtfulness and my heart swelled with love for him. That evening, our lovemaking was more passionate than it had been in a very long time."

It's Not Me

After reading about these people's fantasies, you may be thinking, "Is she kidding? There is no way I could wear a skimpy leather corset or be master of ceremonies in a video love hunt."

There are dozens of reasons why a man or woman may hesitate to create a fantasy for his or her mate. Here are some that I hear over and over again. Do you recognize yourself in any of them?

- I don't have enough imagination.
- I'm not the creative type.
- I don't have enough energy.
- I'm too busy.
- I'm not the romantic type.
- I'm afraid my mate will laugh at me.
- I'm afraid my mate will reject me.
- I'd feel like a phony.

If you are a person who believes you lack imagination or creativity, you've simply lost touch with the playful child inside yourself. All children have imagination and creativity. That quality is still a part of you; you just need to get back in the practice of "make-believe."

If you're afraid that your mate will laugh or dismiss your attempts to create a fantasy as silly, take a deep breath and do it anyway. If they laugh, understand that it's because they aren't used to your new behavior and don't know how to react. Their laughter doesn't signify rejection; it's just a nervous reaction. They're uncomfortable too. To make your fantasy successful, encourage your mate to let go of their normal, analytical self and to pretend along with you. Stay in your role as you persuade them to cooperate, and they won't be able to resist joining in the fun. Inside every man and woman is a little boy or girl dying to come out and play. They just need to be given permission.

If you feel that creating a fantasy for your mate would be phony—that it's not you—I'm asking you to *pretend* that it *is* you. I've got news for you. There isn't any amount of anxiety, nervousness, or discomfort that can't be relieved with the help of daydreaming, fantasizing, and pretending. The mind is an incredible thing. It can take you anyplace you want to go.

I remember lying on a cold, metal table in a hospital room that was the temperature of a refrigerator during one of my radiation treatments. I was absolutely freezing! My teeth were chattering and my fingernails were blue. What got me through that treatment was my ability to pretend that I was lying on a beach on a hot summer day. As my mind worked to create my fantasy, I could actually feel the blood returning to my fingertips.

Soooo . . .

- If you're nervous about showing up at your mate's office with a bouquet of flowers, *pretend* you're an actor or actress worthy of an Academy Award and do it anyway.
- If you think you don't have the energy to plan a surprise theme dinner with music, costumes, and props, *pretend* you have the energy and do it anyway.
- If you think you have no imagination, *pretend* you are the Master Fantasy Creator and have won awards for your productions.
- If you're afraid your mate will laugh at you, *pretend* that nothing ruffles your attempts at loving your mate.

As one of my students, Charlene, learned the first time she created a fantasy for her mate, what happens when we pretend to be someone we're not is that our pretend self takes the place of our real self.

Charlene had worn her poker-straight hair long for the entire twenty-five years that she had been married to Norm. "Norm had hinted several times over the years that he would love to see me with a different hairstyle, but I always dismissed his suggestions. I just couldn't imagine myself any other way."

With the help and encouragement of the other women in class, Charlene, who tended to be shy and withdrawn, imagined herself as perky and bouncy, with short curly hair. There were cries of approval from the class the next week when Charlene walked in looking like a totally different woman. She had cut her hair to shoulder length and had it permed! She beamed as she told us how she surprised her husband at the airport a few days before.

"I was walking toward Norm as he came through the gate," Charlene said. "I was so excited, I felt like I was sixteen again. During the next few seconds my emotions plummeted as I watched my husband walk right by me. I turned around and called his name. I'll never forget Norm's face when he realized who I was. At first he was speechless. Then he couldn't stop talking about how much he loved my new look. My decision to do a makeover has given our marriage a makeover too."

Change Your Image

An important part of creating a fantasy is being able to alter your appearance to fit the theme of your fantasy. If your fantasy has a camping theme, you wouldn't dress in a three-piece suit or an evening gown. Changing your everyday image to fit the fantasy is part of what makes this special time with your mate magical. Dressing the part helps you become the part, and it's vital to your partner's ability to participate in the fantasy. It's a lot easier to respond as if you really are a patient needing medical attention if your doctor is dressed in a white jacket than it would be if he were wearing pajamas! Can you imagine trying to act out a French-maid fantasy in your flannel nightgown?

Dressing up in a costume isn't just for children or for Halloween. You can have fun experimenting any time of the year. One student, Lily, changed her image for her husband every month of the year. With her friend Molly as the photographer, Lily posed for twelve photographs and made a calendar for her husband for Christmas. Between the two of them, Lily and Molly collected enough props and outfits to create a different theme for each month.

"I asked Mitch to take the children to an amusement park for the day," said Lily. "When he asked me why, I told him, 'Trust me. There will be a bigger thrill for you in what I'm doing than any roller coaster you'll ride today.'"

After Mitch left with the kids, Lily and Molly got to work. Her calendar photo shoot went something like this:

JANUARY: Lily holds a glass of champagne as she reclines on the bed wearing a silk teddy and a New Year's Eve party hat.

FEBRUARY: Lily is curled up on their white couch with her arms wrapped around a huge inflated heart that says, "I love you this much." She is wearing a black-and-red teddy, a black garter belt and stockings, and red high-heeled shoes.

MARCH: Lily sits in a wicker chair cuddled up to a white stuffed bunny. She has an Easter basket at her feet. Her little-girl innocence is quite a contrast to her lustful pose for February.

APRIL: Lily again shows her innocent side as she stands by a window wearing a pastel pink nightie and a string of pearls. Her eyes are cast downward toward a single, long-stemmed white rose.

MAY: Lily changes her image for the month of May. Lying on their bedroom floor, she poses seductively in a black lace push-up bra and panties.

JUNE: For Father's Day, Lily perches on a stool wearing her husband's button-down shirt, tie, and bifocals. Mitch's briefcase is at her feet.

JULY: Lily shows her sense of humor as she stands tall—and naked—behind Old Glory, proudly saluting the camera.

AUGUST: Lily wears a bikini as she poses on a beach towel on the deck in their backyard.

SEPTEMBER: Lily sits in their spa up to her shoulders in bubbles.

OCTOBER: Lily is dressed in a black lace teddy, cowboy boots, and a cowboy hat. A fan behind the camera blows the jack-o-lantern wind sock Lily holds in her hand.

NOVEMBER: Dressed in a blue-and-black teddy and black stockings, Lily sits on the piano bench with her upper body reclining on the keys of their upright piano.

DECEMBER: Lily is seen wearing a red teddy and posing in front of their white bedroom door next to a three-foot tall wooden Santa.

When Lily was done with her photo session, she was an expert at changing her image. Mitch loved the calendar and was flabbergasted by it. "To this day, he'll look at me and ask, 'Will you be November?' "

Appealing to the Senses

When producing your mate's fantasy, you want to stimulate as many of the senses as possible. Let your imagination go wild as you pick and choose the kind of lighting, scent, music, clothing, and food you'll need to make your mate's dream come true.

All of Jenny's senses were excited one afternoon when her husband called her home from work for a surprise lunch. It was their tenth wedding anniversary, and Cameron had taken the day off to make his wife's Caribbean fantasy come true.

"We had gone to St. Kitts for our honeymoon and didn't have the funds to get back there for our anniversary, so I decided to bring a little of St. Kitts to Jenny," said Cameron.

Cameron searched the Internet and found a company that sold theme dinner packages, and ordered one with a Caribbean theme. "I've always liked to cook," he said, "so this was a lot of fun. I made black bean soup, a tropical banana drink, pineapple fritters, and Jenny's favorite dessert—key lime pie."

Cameron set up a card table in their bedroom and covered it with a batik print tablecloth and matching napkins. His theme package included a container of flamingo glitter, two inflatable pink flamingos, and two parrots on hanging perches. The company also provided him with two beachcomber hats, two plastic leis, and two pairs of sunglasses. Cameron went the extra mile and found twenty-four feet of palm-tree garland, which he used to decorate their bedroom walls.

"When I heard Jenny's car pull into our garage, I

pulled down our bedroom shades, lighted two citro-
nella candles, and slipped a Jimmy Buffett tape into
the cassette player. When Jenny stepped into our bedroom, she stepped into a tropical paradise."

Harriett was another student who learned that by
creating her mate's fantasies, she would create new
and exciting ways for them to be lovers.

One of Peter's fantasies was to go on an African
safari. With two kids in college, Harriett knew a trip
to another continent was not in their budget, so she
decided to use a little imagination and a lot of creativity to produce a safari right in her own home.

"Prior to Peter's birthday, I spent three weeks
shopping at various home stores to find all the right
accessories to create an African dinner," said Harriett.
She found a five-piece place setting of dishes with
jungle animals on them. She bought a zebra-striped
shower curtain and made it into a tablecloth, and she
purchased cheetah place mats and napkins. She even
found wooden napkin rings carved into the shape of
different African animals.

"Peter's fantasy was truly a labor of love. I hate to
cook," Harriett admitted, "but for Peter I spent seven
hours in the kitchen making Nigerian peanut soup,
cardamom shrimp, and banana fritters. Peter was a
little surprised when he came home from work to
hear jungle drums in the background and find me
wearing the safari jacket and pith helmet I had rented
from a costume shop.

"But when I led him into the dining room, he was
dumbfounded. He assumed I had hired a caterer until
I told him I had done all the cooking, shopping, and
decorating myself.

"Peter rarely shows his emotions," said Harriett, "but I knew I had touched his heart when I saw him wipe away a tear."

Fantasy Under Construction

I've found that creating a fantasy doesn't come as easily for some people as it does for others. That's why I've designed a system to help you produce any fantasy imaginable. Use this system to surprise your mate with his or her dream, or use it to ask for your own fantasy. Picture a fantasy smorgasbord. At the banquet table is a cast of characters, along with a vast selection of different foods, music, settings, clothing, props, and activities. All you have to do is pick and choose the things you'll need to construct the fantasy. Fit all the pieces together and voila! You have created a memory that will last a lifetime. The Create-a-Fantasy system is the smorgasbord. Eat, drink, and be merry.

Cast of Characters

- Policeman
- Fireman
- Repairman
- Doctor
- Test pilot
- Big-game hunter
- Playboy Bunny
- Stripper (male or female)
- Slave
- Harem girl
- French maid
- Manicurist
- Cinderella
- Prince Charming
- Cleopatra
- Fred Astaire
- Ginger Rogers
- Cowboy
- Movie star
- Fashion model
- King Arthur
- Other

Settings

- Your own home
- Your backyard
- At a beach
- In the park
- On a mountain
- At a bar
- In a restaurant
- In a mall
- In a motel
- At an amusement park
- On a boat
- In a plane
- In a tent
- In a car
- Other

Clothing

- Tuxedo
- Belly-dancing costume
- Swimwear
- Western wear
- Lingerie (garter belts, teddies, corsets, stockings, etc.)
- G-strings, silk boxers, bikini briefs
- Silk dressing gown
- Doctor's jacket
- Repairman's uniform
- Policeman's uniform
- Exercise wear (spandex pants, bodysuit)
- Apron
- Nothing but a smile
- Beach towel
- Five-inch heels
- Leather pants, miniskirt, etc.
- Leather chaps
- Evening gown
- Medieval costumes
- Fur coat
- Stick-on bows
- Other

Food

- Chocolate
- Fruit
- Pastries
- Whipped cream
- Honey
- Italian
- Chinese
- Indian
- Arabian
- Caribbean
- Southwestern
- Mexican
- Thai
- French
- Greek
- Cajun
- Other

Music

- Classical
- Jazz
- Show tunes
- Nature sounds
- Hard rock
- Soft rock
- Background music
- Fifties music
- Disco
- Big band
- Other

Props

- Candles
- Romantic board games
- Adult videos
- Gels, lotions, aromatic oils
- Handcuffs
- Water pistol
- Silk scarves
- Whip
- Sex toys
- Adult magazines
- Polaroid camera
- Video camera
- Body paints
- Temporary tattoos
- Feather
- Mirror
- Erotic or romantic literature
- Paper and pens
- Ball of string
- Post-it Notes
- Pillows
- Sheepskin rug
- Red light bulbs
- Colognes, perfumes
- Fireplace
- Dimmer switches
- Makeup
- Nail-care products
- Wigs
- Flowers
- Rose petals
- Violin
- Balloons
- Bubble bath
- Satin sheets
- Other

Activities

- Cooking
- Eating
- Camping
- Belly dancing
- Driving
- Swimming
- Horseback riding
- Flying
- Skiing
- Role playing
- Dancing
- Stripping
- Biking
- Sightseeing
- Photographing
- Shopping
- Hiking
- Drawing
- Boating
- Posing
- Dining out
- Exercising
- Hot-air ballooning
- Ice skating
- In-line skating
- Scuba diving
- Snorkeling
- Rafting
- Other

Many couples have told me they could never have carried out a fantasy without the help of the Create-a-Fantasy system. By scanning the lists they have found the fuel they needed to feed their imaginations and bring their mate's fantasy to life. So that you can see how constructing a fantasy works, let me share with you some stories told to me by men and women who have used the system to inspire them.

A Valentine's Day Surprise

Merle owned a florist shop with his wife, Nanette. It was Valentine's Day, and the two of them were working feverishly making beautiful floral arrangements for their customers. All six phone lines were busy. Every clerk was with a customer, and other clients roamed the shop waiting to be helped.

Suddenly, everyone in the store froze at the sound of a loud voice. A distinguished-looking man walked over to Nanette and announced to everyone that he had been asked by her husband to sing a song to her.

"I was awestruck," said Nanette. "Merle had done some pretty nice things for me in the past, but nothing like this."

As the man belted out "All I Ask of You" from *Phantom of the Opera*, delivery drivers came into the shop to watch, patrons drew nearer, and phone customers held off placing orders so they could listen in on this romantic moment. "I was crying and blowing my nose long after the song was over," Nanette recalls. Employees who witnessed the performance talked about it all afternoon. Nanette, who was usually strictly business during a holiday, couldn't stop smiling.

Then it happened. Another interruption!

This time two young men entered the store. One was pushing a cart and the other was carrying a violin case. As the man with the cart set up a small table and covered it with a long white tablecloth, the other man took out his violin and began to play "The Music of the Night," also from *Phantom*.

"One of the men came into my office and escorted me to the table," said Nanette. "He then proceeded to light the candles, pour me a glass of wine, and serve me an elegant meal."

"I was watching the whole thing from the back of the store," said Merle. "Timing was critical. I don't know what I would have done if Nanette had decided to go to the bank and hadn't been there." At the perfect moment, Merle appeared before his wife, presented her with a single red rose, and asked her to dance.

"There we were, in the middle of our flower shop, dancing," remembers Nanette. "Phones rang and customers stared, but I was oblivious. I was in a fairy tale in a land far, far away."

Believe it or not, all of Merle's ideas for the fantasy were triggered by the word "violin" in the Create-a-Fantasy props list. "I don't think I ever could have been so creative if I hadn't had the list of ideas to choose from," he said. "I surprised Nanette with another fantasy six months later, on our anniversary. I'm getting really good at this."

A Bed of Roses

Madeline also used the Create-a-Fantasy system to construct a fantasy for her husband. Madeline had known for a long time that one of Burt's fantasies was for her to take the initiative sexually. Throughout the years, it had always been Burt who had to approach her, never the reverse.

After looking over the lists of props and activities, Madeline got an idea.

"I was so nervous," said Madeline. "I checked off all the things I needed, but I walked around with my list in my pocket for two days before I finally decided to do it. I knew how much it would mean to Burt."

What did Madeline decide to do? She decided to take charge!

From the list of props, Madeline chose handcuffs and a water pistol. With props in hand, she marched into her husband's office during his lunch hour, pointed the gun at Burt, and said, "You're under arrest. You're coming with me."

As Madeline slapped the handcuffs on Burt's wrists, he got a funny grin on his face and asked, "But Officer, what did I do?"

"It's not what you've done, but what you're about to do that I'm arresting you for," Madeline replied. She led Burt out of his office and onto the elevator. Burt's colleague Kenneth happened to be on the elevator, too. Kenneth raised an eyebrow at Burt, but said nothing.

"Kenneth, this is my wife, Madeline," said Burt, grinning. "We have a lunch date today." Kenneth nodded with a look that was part embarrassment and part envy.

Once home, Madeline led Burt to their bedroom, where she had prepared a lunch hour of lovemaking. Spread across their bed were rose petals and an array of silk scarves. Madeline looked into Burt's eyes and told him, "Life with you has always been a bed of roses. To thank you, I'd like to make love to you on them."

Burt was beside himself. His fantasy had finally come true.

Time Out for Love

Clark made his wife's fantasy become a reality by using two simple household items he picked from the

Create-a-Fantasy lists: a ball of string and Post-it Notes.

Jill and Clark had extremely busy schedules, and one of Jill's fantasies was that Clark would stop in the middle of their hectic life to show her how much he loved her. He did just that.

It was 6:15 on a weeknight. Clark had stopped on his way home from work to pick up a pizza that he and Jill were going to eat before they rushed off to their respective meetings. On that particular night, their conversation went something like this:

> Clark (*entering the house with the pizza*): Here's the pizza. It's still pretty hot. We better let it cool off before we eat it.
>
> Jill: I don't have time to let it cool off. My meeting starts at seven. Yours doesn't start until eight, right?
>
> Clark: Right. So how did work go today?
>
> Jill (*looking at the clock*): Oh my gosh, I've got to go or I'll be late. (*Jill grabs her coat and a piece of pizza and gives Clark a quick kiss.*) I'll see you later.

As Clark listened to Jill's car pull out of the driveway, he decided to do something that he had been thinking about for a while. He wanted to show Jill how important she was to him, and he knew just how he was going to do it. He found a ball of string and tied one end to the back doorknob with a note attached that said, "Follow the string." He pulled the string to the coat closet and wrapped it around an empty hanger with a note that said, "Hang up your coat." Then Clark unraveled the string over the teapot, which sat alongside a cup containing a tea bag. He attached a note that said, "Have a cup of tea—and me." Clark continued his "love web" until he finished it upstairs in the bedroom, where he set up a candlelit table, a bottle of wine, and two wine glasses. His final note said, "Turn around to find the person who adores you."

In a very short amount of time and with the help of some simple household items, Clark created a fantasy Jill will treasure for a lifetime.

Rendezvous with a Stranger

Sophie used more than a few household items to create a fantasy for her husband, Stu, but all her preparation was worth the effort. Stu had always talked about wanting Sophie to role-play being someone she wasn't.

"I majored in theater in college," said Sophie, "but somehow acting a part for Stu seemed too uncomfortable. It wasn't until I saw the Create-a-Fantasy system that I mustered up the courage to playact for him."

For Stu's birthday Sophie decided to dress completely opposite to the way she normally dresses. A brunette, Sophie borrowed a neighbor's blond Eva Gabor wig. She borrowed a short black leather skirt from another friend. Sophie rarely wore makeup or accessories, but for this special occasion, she went all the way with the eye shadow, blush, lipstick, and jewelry. The day of her surprise, Sophie called Stu's administrative assistant and asked her to leave Stu a phone message saying that a woman who refused to leave her name had called and requested that he meet her at the restaurant in a local hotel at 6:00 P.M.

"When I left our kids at the baby-sitter's, our four-year-old asked me if it was Halloween," laughed Sophie. "On the way to the restaurant I began to sweat. 'Do I really look ready to go trick-or-treating?' I wondered. Then I began to worry as what I had done dawned on me. 'What if Stu thinks it is a strange woman he's meeting, instead of me? What if that's the reason he comes?' I worried.

"Finally, I forced myself to stop the second-guessing and concentrated on how much Stu was going to love this. I arrived at the hotel with time to spare, and as I walked into the lobby and made my way to the lounge, I noticed I was attracting quite a few stares. By the time I sat down, my heart was pounding and my legs felt like Jell-O.

"Just as I was beginning to worry again about Stu coming to meet a strange woman and trying to decide how I felt about that possibility, he walked into the lounge. With an anticipatory, but rather tense look on his face, his eyes scanned the room. He looked past me once and then did a double take. I waved to him coquettishly as he walked slowly toward me with his mouth hanging open.

" 'Hey there, big boy. Pull up a chair and sit awhile,' I said in my best Mae West voice. Stu looked shocked as he asked, 'What did you do? What is all this?'

"I kissed him and said, 'Happy birthday, honey.'

"Stu shook his head, looked at me with tears in his eyes, and said, 'You did all this for me?'

" 'Not only that, I have a room reserved for us

upstairs.' I replied, feeling very proud of myself that I had pulled the whole thing off."

Another woman told me that she had created a fantasy for her husband's thirty-eighth birthday using the Create-a-Fantasy lists. "I took my husband to a nice restaurant to celebrate. After dinner I slipped into the bathroom, changed into a slinky black dress, then returned to the table and sang 'Happy Birthday, Mr. President' à la Marilyn Monroe to my husband in this crowded restaurant. He loved it."

A Scenario for Fun

If you're still hesitant after looking through the Create-a-Fantasy lists and reading about how others have used them, I've got one more trick up my sleeve to help you step into the realm of the imagination. What follows are several scenarios, each derived from a single source of inspiration. Use these scenarios to trigger your fantasy.

Use Stationery

Stationery can be used to invite your mate to any event imaginable. For example, for your anniversary, you could send your mate a wedding invitation to his or her own wedding. Explain that you loved marrying him or her so much the first time that you want to do it again. Attach a questionnaire asking who should be included on the guest list, what type of attire would be appropriate, where the ceremony should be held, and any other questions you like. Let your partner know that you are taking care of all the details. All he or she has to do is say, "I do."

Use Technology

Tell your mate to clear his or her schedule to have a private conference with you. Explain that you have a lot of things to discuss on the agenda. Use today's technology of phone, fax, or E-mail to describe in great detail a sexual fantasy you have planned for him or her. Tell your mate that the deadline for this project is tonight. No doubt your mate won't stop thinking about you all day and will arrive home early.

Use Toys

Playing with toys brings out the irresistible kid in us. Take a trip to a toy store and buy some magic tricks. Game companies make a magic hat that includes a wand, white gloves, and several easy-to-learn magic tricks. Practice your magic show until you have it mastered, then entertain and dazzle your mate with your newly acquired skills. Halfway into your act, ask your mate to be your assistant. Tell him or her that you have to step out of the room for a moment. Return nude and tell your mate it's your new disappearing act. Then invite your assistant to your bedroom to teach him or her some new tricks.

Use Food

Prepare a favorite meal that includes at least four courses. Instead of feeding yourselves, you and your mate must feed each other. As your mate feeds you with a fork, spoon, and his or her fingers, sensuously lick everything clean. End your evening by watching the video of the movie *Tom Jones,* in which there is an erotic eating scene. Before the movie ends, you'll be hungry for each other.

Use Your Body

Your body is a wonderful vehicle for expressing your love for your mate. A week in advance, tell your mate that you have tickets for a hot new show in town, but don't say what it is. A few days before the show, send a homemade ticket to your mate with a pretend playbill explaining that the show begins in your bedroom at a specific time. When your mate arrives, he or she will be entertained and aroused by your own personal strip show. Explain to your partner that audience members can look, but not touch (until after the performance), and that tipping is encouraged.

Use Water

Water can be one of the most sensual methods for creating a fantasy. Fill your bathtub with warm water and bubble bath. Invite your mate to join you in a relaxing bath. Cup your hands, fill them with water, and pour it over different parts of your mate's body. Gently rinse the soap off each other, as you delight in the pleasure of water play.

Use Nature

Nature—its sights, its sounds, and its smells—offers a wonderful opportunity for you and your mate to create a fantasy. Take your mate on a nature hike in the woods. You are the tour guide. As you and your mate follow the trail, point out the different types of vegetation. Tell your mate that for a small fee you will take only the most evolved naturalists on a private tour of rare flowers and trees. As you take this informative side trip, you are quick to spot any secluded areas and let nature take its course.

The K.I.S.S. Plan

In any long-term relationship there will be times when it becomes routine. If you let too much time pass without changing the routine, the relationship will become boring. Before this happens in your relationship, **K**eep **I**t **S**omething **S**pecial by taking time to create a fantasy for your mate.

The first step is to look at the lists from my Create-a-Fantasy system. Construct your mate's fantasy by selecting what you need from the lists of places, clothing, food, music, props, and activities.

The second step is for you to sit quietly, close your eyes, and follow your imagination wherever it leads you. Give your imagination a little nudge by thinking about romantic encounters you've shared in the past. Then use that mental energy to fantasize about what you think your mate would like to see happen in the future. Play the fantasy out in your mind to completion. Remember, there are no limits to making someone's fantasy come true.

The third and final step is to pick a time, set the scene, and take your mate to fantasyland!

7
THE THREE-MINUTE QUICKIE

I remember the exact moment when I realized for the first time that I really was an adult. My husband and I were on vacation in Las Vegas and were seated in a restaurant, about to have dinner. Suddenly, I craved an ice-cream sundae. My immediate thought was, "Ellen, you can't have a sundae now. Sundaes are for dessert. You have never in your life eaten dessert before dinner." Then I did the unthinkable. I ordered the sundae and ate it before dinner. I remember thinking, "I am an adult. If I want a sundae before dinner, I can have one." It was so exhilarating to act on impulse and do what I wanted to do, in spite of my childhood programming. I was thirty years old the day I declared my independence by having dessert before dinner.

What does having an ice-cream sundae have to do

with having a quickie? For me, it was the first step in recovering the spontaneity I had as a child. Sex doesn't always have to be orchestrated or anticipated to be good. Sometimes, just a few moments stolen out of the hectic routine of daily life can make a couple feel close. When your relationship is good and you have an otherwise fulfilling and satisfying sex life, having a "quickie" can be lustfully fun. Those times can have an added intensity that increases the pleasure of a quick embrace enough to make it worth the risk of being interrupted.

Indulging in a quickie is difficult for some people. It means acting on impulse, being spontaneous, maybe even taking a risk—all of which go against what we were taught as we were growing up. As children, we were naturally impulsive. When children get the urge to do something, they do it. If they ask for something, they expect to get it at once. Part of growing up is learning to delay gratification. Our parents made us wait for dessert until we had finished our meal. We had to do our chores before we could play. If we wanted to go to a friend's house, we had to do our homework first.

We continue this pattern as adults. Some people postpone having children until they are financially ready or emotionally mature enough. Many people delay buying a home until they can afford the one they want. Stifling our impulses and delaying gratification are part of being a responsible adult. On the other hand, being an adult also means knowing when it's okay to be impulsive. Part of being a "grown-up" is being able to let the child in you come out to play when it's appropriate. If you're the type of person who finds it difficult to be spontaneous, having a quickie will probably be a stretch for you at first. You might have to practice being spontaneous in some less daring situations. The following exercise is just one way to practice being more spontaneous. This is a great adventure for people who always have to plan ahead. If you're one of those people who would never dream of getting in the car without an address and a map, let go for one day and see how free you feel.

Set aside a day to be alone with your mate: no children, no friends, no neighbors, no relatives, just the two of you. Do not have an agenda. Get in your car and start driving, with no destination in mind. Stop whenever you feel like it. Eat whenever you feel like it. Stop to admire the view, walk on the sand, take a short hike, or explore those interesting side roads you've always wondered about. Whatever you do, enjoy it to the fullest by staying in the moment. Model your mood after that carefree quality of childhood, leaving thoughts of unfinished business or other obligations behind.

It's not necessary to spend an entire day to practice being spontaneous. There are many opportunities in the course of daily life when you could give in to temptation without dire results. For instance, the next time you pass the cosmetic counter in a department store, take time for the makeup technician to give you a makeover. I'll bet you've thought of it a million times, but you've always thought, "Not today. I haven't got time." Well, next time just do it!

How about that special tool you've always wanted, but never allowed yourself to buy? It's really not that expensive, but you've never really needed it, either. You probably thought, "I'll buy it when I need it." Why not buy it now, and have the fun of knowing it's hanging in your garage in case you need it in the future?

Be spontaneous. Indulge yourself a little. It's really okay to give yourself permission to break out of your adult habit of being responsible twenty-four hours a day, seven days a week. I promise you, the world won't come to an end, and you'll begin to feel more lighthearted about life in general. The more you practice being spontaneous, the easier it will be for you to give in to the urge to have a quickie when the thought comes into your mind.

Here and Now

I know that at least occasionally you have an impulsive, lustful thought about your mate. I can assure you that you're not alone. I've been told by hundreds of men and women that they sometimes think about how much fun a quickie might be, but instead of putting their thoughts into action, all too often they sabotage their impulse by saying to themselves, "Better not. This isn't a good time," or "Uh-uh. It wouldn't be appropriate." You probably already know that if you always stifle your impulse, waiting to make love until the perfect time, your sex life will wither and die on the vine. Now is the perfect time! This is the perfect place!

Practice being spontaneous in as many ways as possible, and eventually when the impulse to have a quickie hits you, you will be able to act on it just as easily as the couple whose story follows. This is how one of my students recalls a recent afternoon, which included a quickie for her husband and herself.

"As I removed my crystal stemware from the dining-room hutch, I heard my husband, Tom, trudging up the basement stairs with two cases of soft drinks in his arms. It was Saturday afternoon and we were busy working in our home, putting together another night of entertaining.

"As much as we love to entertain, preparing for the party can be a drag. By the time our guests arrive, we often feel like restaurant owners hosting a grand opening. On this particular afternoon, we were exhausted and certainly didn't feel close to one another," Amy said.

She went on to tell me that she was tired of spending a day off from work focusing on another "event" rather than on her husband. The closest they got to making a physical connection was when Tom handed Amy the card table.

As Amy put the finishing touches on the relish tray, she realized the house was silent. She did a quick inventory of her children to verify that their one-year-old was down for a nap, and their seven-year-old daughter, Laura, had just left to play next door. Amy suddenly got a flash of inspiration.

Amy (*tiptoeing through the house, whispering):* Tom? Tom, where are you?
Tom (*coming up from the basement):* I'm right here. Why are you whispering?
Amy: Listen, do you hear anything?
Tom: No, why?

Amy: Do you know what this means?

Tom *(recognizing the sparkle in Amy's eyes):* Do we have time?

Amy: Sure we do. Jessica just fell asleep and Laura's next door playing.

Like two little kids sneaking off to do something forbidden, Amy and Tom ran upstairs to their bedroom. In the middle of their intimate time together, they heard the front door open. In unison, they whispered, "Laura's home!" As they scrambled to put their clothes back on, they gave each other a wink, knowing that they'd feel connected for the rest of the day.

Amy and Tom are a perfect example of a couple who know how to seize the moment. Amy honored her spur-of-the-moment desire for her husband in the middle of a busy day, and acting on her feelings gave her and Tom an opportunity to feel close and connected.

Another couple who have learned the value of occasional impulsive behavior are Peggy and Neil, who have owned a retail business for sixteen years. Since they are unable to have children, their business is their baby. "I'm in charge of personnel and purchasing, and Neil handles all the marketing and public relations," says Peggy.

"After taking the *Light His Fire* class, I was inspired to surprise Neil with a quickie. I just wasn't sure where and when to spring it on him," she said.

Then one day, while the two of them were working in their corporate office, Peggy felt a surge of spontaneity and sexuality in the same moment. Neil was talking with the office manager when Peggy went up to him and said, "Excuse me, Neil, but may I see you in the conference room for a minute?"

"Sure," said Neil.

"Hold all of our calls for a few minutes, please," Peggy told their office manager.

Neil followed Peggy into the conference room, and watched her as she closed and locked the door. "What's going on?" he asked.

With a single stroke of her arm, Peggy swept all of the papers that were spread across the conference table onto the floor, and said, "Neil, drop your pants. It's time for a break!"

Neil says, "Now whenever someone says, 'Just lay it on the conference table,' or 'Why don't we do it in the conference room?' I look at Peggy and we both crack up."

Another student couldn't suppress her sexual impulses when visiting the zoo one day with her husband. Fran's favorite exhibit at the zoo was called Monkey Island. This exhibit, shaped like a mountain, had rocks jutting out in all different directions so that the monkeys could jump from one level to the next.

Fran and her husband, Don, had spent at least an hour watching the monkeys. "I don't know what it is that's so appealing about monkeys," said Fran, "I'm just so enthralled with their behavior."

A few minutes before closing time, Fran noticed two monkeys flirting with each other. "Look, Don, look how cute they are," said Fran.

"They look more angry than cute," said Don. "I think we're intruding on their togetherness. Come on, let's go."

"Wait a minute," said Fran, grabbing Don's hand and leading him to a remote spot behind a big rock. In the few minutes they had before closing time they brought a whole new meaning to the term *monkey business.*

Follow the Leader

In every class I teach, in every lecture I give, in every seminar I conduct, there are always people who are shocked or outraged by the idea of a quickie. "A quickie might be fine for a man, but I need time to really enjoy sex," a woman will say. Another person will make the comment that they'd be too tense to have sex if they felt they might be caught at any moment. I understand completely. After years of being responsible adults and confining our lovemaking to the bedroom, becoming spontaneous and adventurous about sex takes a lot of practice. Even though as young lovers we may have made love anyplace we thought we could get away with it, as adults we tend to enjoy the comforts of a king-size bed and the security of a locked door. I always remind these people that it's important to their relationship to keep the spark alive with spontaneous sex.

It's often true that one person in a partnership is more naturally spontaneous than the other. If you are the more inhibited and cautious partner, for the sake of your relationship, allow your mate the pleasure of being your coach in encouraging you to try something new. If, on the other hand, you are the more daring and impulsive one, gently and lovingly encourage your mate to be a little more adventurous.

It's not at all unusual for the same people who objected to the idea of a quickie when I talked about it in class or a lecture, to come back at a later date to tell me they've followed my advice and are happy that they did. Almost always, they then go on to share their stories with me.

A Romp in the Garden

In this case, Marguerite followed Christopher's cues while they were visiting an art museum one summer day. Sculpting was one of their favorite hobbies, and they loved to spend an afternoon strolling in the sculpture garden. They'd gaze at the mammoth statues of the Greek gods and goddesses, and often draw sketches of what they saw.

"One day, in the middle of sketching a particularly shapely female form, Christopher looked at me and decided we had to make love right then and there," Marguerite disclosed.

"I knew the garden like the back of my hand," said Christopher. "We had been there so many times. I knew there was a secluded alcove at the end of the garden. There was only one small sculpture there, and most people missed it because it was so out of the way. I quietly suggested we make love inside the alcove."

"At first I was absolutely mortified at the thought and I refused," said Marguerite. "It's not that I wasn't excited by the idea, but I was afraid of getting caught.

But Christopher was so reassuring that I was finally convinced it was safe."

"Marguerite and I sneaked into the alcove, and I pulled a potted ficus tree in front of the alcove to ensure that no one would see us," said Christopher.

"As short as it was, our lovemaking was incredible," said Marguerite. "The possibility of getting caught made it extremely intense. As it happened, no one even came by, so I'll be a lot easier to convince the next time Christopher feels adventurous."

Nauti-*cal Nooner*

In Marie and Gene's case, Marie was the leader, and Gene was the follower. This couple lived in the Northeast and were ready for a tropical vacation. They had just had twenty-two inches of snow dumped on them, and they were getting cabin fever.

Gene came home the week after the big storm with tickets for the last two seats on a flight going to the Caribbean island of St. Martin. They had been to St. Martin in the past, and for the next few days they looked forward eagerly to sunning on the beautiful beaches. After they arrived, they found a favorite beach and went there every day. As usual, they swam in the ocean whenever the sun got too hot for them.

One day around lunchtime, Gene and Marie were having a good time floating and bobbing in the warm ocean when Marie swam up to Gene and whispered in his ear, "What do you think?"

"What do I think about what?"

"You know," said Marie. "How about a little . . . you know."

Astonished, Gene said, "With all those people sitting on the beach?"

"Look at them," said Marie. "They're not paying any attention to us. They're all concentrating on their tans."

"I don't know about this," said Gene doubtfully.

But before Gene had a chance to object further, Marie had shed her bathing suit and was rubbing her bare skin against Gene's.

It was too much for Gene to resist. "You talked me into it," he said as he took her into his arms and kissed her.

That afternoon, cruising the Caribbean took on a whole new meaning for Gene and Marie. And Marie was right. No one on the beach gave them a second glance. Only the fish knew their secret.

Keeping Secrets

Part of the mystique of a quickie can be its somewhat illicit overtones. Keeping your passionate interlude a secret adds excitement to the event. Remember when you were a teenager and had to sneak a chance to make out with your boyfriend or girlfriend? Whether you hid behind the garage, snuck down to the basement, or slipped away to the attic, the element of danger added a thrill to your encounters that may be missing now that you are adults. Although you are older now, it is possible for you and your mate to recapture that old feeling. All you have to do is sneak a chance to make love without your children catching on.

"With a nine-year-old and an eleven-year-old, finding time to make love is a challenge in our household," said Ed. "We're always on the run—taking the children to soccer tournaments, swim meets, and dance classes, so Julie and I have to sneak our time together. We have a regular date to mate on Sunday mornings in the shower of our master suite while the kids are watching cartoons. The kids are completely unaware. Our shower meeting is our little secret."

When they had their bathroom remodeled recently, Julie and Ed had a nice, wide seat built into the wall for their weekly date. When one of the kids asked her why they had a seat installed, Julie simply replied, "Storage, honey, storage."

Even though they're adults and have been married for several years, Nina and Henry still sneak behind their parents' backs. They both come from large families who live some distance away. As a result, they frequently have out-of-town visitors.

Last Thanksgiving Nina and Henry's house was overflowing with family. Nina's parents, Henry's parents, and four of their cousins came to stay for several days. Nina and Henry hadn't had any time alone together in days, and it was beginning to get them down. On Thanksgiving Day, everyone gathered in the family room after dinner to watch a movie.

Nina and Henry looked longingly at each other from across the room. Nina noticed that everyone was focused on the movie, so she motioned for Henry to follow her as she snuck out of the room and went up the stairs to their bedroom. Once in the bedroom,

Nina opened the door to their closet and pulled Henry inside.

"What are we doing in our closet?" asked Henry.

"I figured this was the only place we could make love without anyone walking in on us," Nina told him.

"Then why do they call it a walk-in closet?" Henry asked.

"Very funny, Henry. Just be quiet and kiss me," Nina giggled.

From that point on, their closet became Nina and Henry's secret hiding place whenever they needed to escape the togetherness of family visits.

Peephole Alert

Either some people are more adventurous than others, or they're just plain desperate. Tony and his wife saw a window of opportunity to have a most exciting and suspenseful sexual encounter that would never have occurred to most couples.

Their son was to be picked up at 7:00 P.M. to go to a movie, and their daughter was due to return home at 7:00 P.M. from a birthday party.

At 7:00 sharp, their son's ride arrived. Now the question was, Should they take a chance that their daughter would be late getting home, and risk a quickie? Past history told them the odds were in their favor.

Martha put her arms around Tony's neck, let herself lean back against the door, and pulled Tony to her. That was more than enough convincing for Tony.

Just when it seemed like they were going to get away with their little romantic adventure, Tony's eye came level with the peephole. There was their daughter getting out of a car.

"Oh no, she's coming," Tony groaned.

"Well, at least somebody is," laughed Martha.

Clueless in Cleveland

Another couple were daring enough to sneak behind their children's backs when they were less than twenty feet away.

"It was a hot summer's night and all of the fans in our home were going," said Anna. "Our kids were sprawled across the family-room floor like slugs, watching a video they had been begging to see for days."

While the kids watched the movie, Anna and Doug sat in the living room, complaining about the heat and humidity. Suddenly a devilish smile spread across Doug's face.

"What are you thinking?" asked Anna.

"I'm thinking it would be a lot cooler on our screened-in porch than it is in here," said Doug.

"Okay," said Anna. "Let's go out there."

As she got up to walk to the porch, Doug grabbed her arm and pulled her onto his lap. "Let's make love out there," he whispered.

"Are you crazy," said Anna. "What about the kids?"

"Their eyes are glued to the TV," said Doug. "Come on. They'll never know."

Doug and Anna snuck out to the porch and made a little heat of their own, while the kids remained clueless in the family room.

Dare to Be Different

Having a quickie in your own home is wonderful, but if you really want to feel a rush of adrenaline, have a quickie in a totally outrageous place. Dare to be different!

On a recent trip, Alicia and Carmine unwittingly became members of a very exclusive club. They were flying the red-eye from California to Chicago, and were two of only twenty-seven passengers on board the plane.

"It was around three-thirty A.M. and I had been dozing for about an hour," said Alicia. "Suddenly, I felt Carmine shaking my arm. He leaned over and whispered, 'Alicia, I want to make love to you.' I told him he must be dreaming, but he got out of his seat and motioned me toward the bathroom."

"I know Alicia thought I'd lost my mind," said Carmine. "But I had taken a head count and knew that everyone had dozed off. We could make love in the bathroom and no one would ever know."

"It must have been the altitude," said Alicia. "I felt like a giddy teenager again. It may be the most exciting thing Carmine and I have ever done. As an added bonus, the bathrooms were by the engine, so no one could hear us. We could make as much noise as we wanted."

"The rest of the trip was wonderful. We went back

to our seats, and fell asleep in each other's arms," said Carmine. "We had no idea we had become members of the Mile-High Club until we heard someone talking about it on the radio a couple of months later."

Shop Till You Drop

Carla and Jerry had been out looking at open houses and were on their way home from what had been a long, exhausting day when Carla remembered she needed a new pair of jeans. Carla knew Jerry hated to shop, but she needed the jeans for that evening. They had a date with friends to go dancing at a local country-and-western club, and the only jeans she had were too tight.

"I promise, Jerry, we'll just go to the one store. I won't even look in any of the other store windows. It'll only take a few minutes," she begged.

They parked the car and hurried into the mall to make a quick purchase. Once inside the store, Carla quickly selected several pairs of jeans and took them to a dressing room to try them on. After a short time, she poked her head out of the dressing-room door and motioned to Jerry to come inside to help her decide which jeans were the most flattering.

When Jerry was inside, Carla said, "Look, Jerry," and pointed to a raised platform in front of the mirrors.

"What's that for?" asked Jerry.

"It's to sit on, silly. They make these jeans so tight, it's impossible to step into them. You have to sort of sit down, lie back, raise your legs, and wriggle into them. That's what that platform's for. But . . . I have a better idea," Carla said as she reached behind Jerry and locked the door to the dressing room.

"Here, honey, help me get out of these jeans," Carla said as she reclined suggestively on the platform.

Jerry took her cue and they enjoyed a very hot time in the old mall that night.

"Now when Carla asks me to go shopping with her, I jump at the chance," Jerry says.

No Frills

There are times when lovemaking occurs after hours of preparation. Showers are taken. Aftershave, cologne, perfume, or dusting powder is applied. Music and lighting are chosen to set the mood.

With a quickie, there's no time to primp or spruce up. You look like you look, you smell like you smell, and setting the scene is not a concern because you are where you are.

"Years ago, when John had his hernia operation, they kept people in the hospital for a week," Evelyn recalled as she told me the following story.

"We'd only been married two months when John had to have surgery. It was devastating to be apart for so long. I visited him at the hospital twice a day and stayed as long as they would let me.

"I remember sitting by his bed, massaging his arms and legs as I told him how much he meant to me," said Evelyn.

"I wasn't looking my best," added John. "My hair

hadn't been washed in days and I smelled like a hospital. But after five days of Evelyn's massages I couldn't stand it anymore.

"I'd gotten to know some of the other men on the floor and I talked them into buzzing the nurses all at the same time one night so that Evelyn and I could have a few minutes to make love. I didn't look the way I would have liked and the atmosphere was less than romantic, but our quickie kept us feeling close and connected until I could come home from the hospital," John said.

Here's another story about seizing the moment, no matter where you are or how you look.

After golfing seventeen holes, Alice and her husband Sam were better prepared to hit the showers than to hit the hay. "We were teeing up for the eighteenth hole," said Alice. "It was a pretty easy shot, right down the middle, with woods along the left side of the fairway. I walked up to the tee and hit my ball straight for the woods.

"Sam looked at me in amazement and said, 'Alice, what in the devil are you doing? You hit the ball right into the woods.'

" 'Come on,' I said with a grin on my face. 'Let's go find my ball.' We got in the golf cart and drove to the woods. Although my hair was a mess and my makeup was running, I led Sam into the middle of the trees, took off my clothes, and said, 'I've always wanted to make love to you on this golf course.'

"Whenever we play that course with our friends, Sam mentions the time he made a hole in one on the eighteenth hole. They all think he's joking."

The More the Merrier

Some couples find it exciting to have a quickie while other people are close by. Making love while other people are in the immediate vicinity but oblivious to your sexual encounter can be quite stimulating.

That's what Joy and Ben discovered at one of their family gatherings. "We were with the kids at my in-laws' house for a Fourth of July picnic one year," said Joy. "I don't know why, but whenever we visit Ben's parents, there always seems to be a conflict of some kind. This time, the family couldn't agree on which fireworks were okay to shoot off, and which ones the city deemed unsafe for residential use.

"At one point there was so much tension that Ben and I decided to slip away and be alone. Ben's parents have a beautiful Japanese garden and in the center of it is a small building designed like a Japanese teahouse. While everyone was debating about which fireworks to use, Ben and I set off some fireworks of our own.

"There were no lights in the teahouse, just the moonlight shining through the doorway. It was so exciting and romantic to make love there, knowing that the family was just a few feet away and unaware that we were missing. By the time we were finished, the fireworks debate was settled, but Ben and I were still glowing."

The Top Ten

In the seventeen years that I've been teaching couples how to improve their relationships, I've heard hundreds of stories about the different ways people find to fit a quickie into their busy lives, or to use a quickie to enliven their relationship when it begins to become routine. You've already read a lot of these stories in the preceding pages. What follows are ten of my favorites.

1. Around the Block

Leah, a woman who had listened to my tape program, wrote to tell me the story of what she called a "reuniting quickie."

She and a girlhood friend had been on a three-day cruise to the Bahamas while her husband, Lou, stayed home and took care of the children. This was the first time that Leah and Lou had been away from each other since their marriage six years before.

"I think it was harder on Lou than on me," Leah wrote. "I missed him, but I had a lot of exciting things to do to keep my mind occupied. When my girlfriend and I got off the plane, Lou and the kids were waiting for me at the gate. I cried when I saw Lou standing there waiting for me, holding a single rose in his hand. Until that moment, I hadn't realized how very much I had missed him."

On the way home from the airport, Lou and Leah couldn't stop looking at each other hungrily. Leah's girlfriend picked up on their signals, and when Lou pulled the car in the driveway she offered to take their two little ones for a drive around the neighborhood.

"I had to laugh as I pictured my girlfriend driving around and around the block so Lou and I could be alone," said Leah. "To this day, I am so grateful to her for her perceptiveness. Those few minutes were among the most passionate moments Lou and I have ever experienced together."

2. Our Spa-cial Time Together

Sue and her husband recently bought a spa for their back deck. "I get really bad back spasms and the spa we bought has great therapeutic jets," said Sue.

What Sue didn't realize when they bought the spa was that she would get more exercise than relaxation when using it. "Roy and I love to use the spa when the kids aren't around, and inevitably, we end up having a quickie," said Sue. "I don't know if it's the temperature of the water or the pulsating movement that makes us want to make love, but whatever it is, I like it a lot!"

3. Not the Welcome Wagon

Charles and Doris love camping. When they were younger, they did a lot of tent camping, but now that they are senior citizens, they camp in their motor home.

"We call it our love nest on wheels," said Doris. "We take lots of short trips and meet friends we've made on previous camping trips at our favorite campgrounds."

Doris and Charles also enjoy golf and tennis and try to incorporate both wherever they camp. "With all the activities we enjoy, we keep very busy during the day," said Charles. "Every once in a while, I like to take a break from our busy schedule and coax Doris back to the motor home for a quickie."

"I used to feel so self-conscious about being in our motor home in broad daylight with all the shades drawn," said Doris. "I was sure everyone would know what we were doing. I guess they didn't, because a couple of times, someone would knock on the door to see if we were all right. After that, I worried that we would forget to lock the door and one of them would come in."

"I took care of that," said Charles. "I made up a laminated sign to hang on the door that says, 'If you see our home a rockin', please don't come a knockin'.' " Doris and Charles haven't had unwanted visitors since.

4. A Drive on the Wild Side

On Fred's fiftieth birthday his wife wanted to do something extra special for him. Since neither of them had ever ridden in a limousine, Joni arranged to have a limousine pick Fred up after work and drive him home in style. When the driver pulled up to Fred's house, Joni was sitting on their front porch all dressed up and ready for a night on the town. Before Fred had a chance to get out of the car, the driver had opened the back door for Joni.

"Happy birthday, Freddy," Joni said as she slid into the seat next to him. Fred's eyes were big as saucers and his mouth hung open in shock. As the limousine pulled out of their driveway, Joni said, "Driver, privacy window, please."

In the rearview mirror, Fred saw the driver smile as the privacy window closed. "Where are we going?" Fred asked Joni when he finally found his voice.

"We're going to have fun, that's where we're going," said Joni, as she began to unbuckle her husband's belt. Fred anxiously looked out the long windows that stretched along the length of the limousine. "Don't worry," Joni reassured him, "We can see out, but no one can see in."

It didn't take Fred much time at all to relax and go along for the ride.

5. Drama in the Darkroom

Brenda has fond memories of her father-in-law showing her how to develop film in his basement darkroom when she and Leon were first dating. "I was so amazed to see a picture gradually appear out of nothing, right before my eyes," said Brenda.

However, those memories pale in comparison to the memories she and Leon created in that same darkroom a few years after they were married.

"I'll never forget the first time we 'did it' in the darkroom," said Leon. "We were at my parents' house for Thanksgiving dinner. Mom asked me to go down to the cellar and get her a can of cranberries. Right after I got downstairs, Brenda followed me to tell me that Mom wanted two cans instead of one."

As they passed the darkroom, Brenda said, "Gosh, it's been so long since I was in there developing film with your dad."

That's when Leon got creative and said, "Let's go develop a little somethin' right now, baby."

"Oh, stop it, you bad boy," laughed Brenda.

"Before I knew it," Brenda said, "Leon and I were making love in total darkness. Let me tell you, it's a very different experience than making love with the lights off in your bedroom. There's just something about a darkroom that's amazing!"

6. Let's Make a Deal

Art and Jeneen were car shopping one day when Jeneen got really racy. "We wanted to trade in our sedate sedan for a sportier car," said Jeneen. "After we had shopped around for several months, I decided that I wanted a red Volkswagen convertible. Art thought the Volkswagen was well made, but he wanted a car with more trunk space for his camping equipment.

"The day we were at the dealership, I saw the exact car that I wanted. It was parked four rows back from the street in the parking lot. I begged Art to look at it with me. I convinced the car salesman that Art and I needed a few minutes alone in the car to see how it felt, and I asked him for the key.

"When Art and I got to the car, I asked him to sit in the back seat with me to see how much leg room there would be for passengers. The minute he sat down, I put my arms around him and said, "I want to make love to you in this car."

" 'In this car that we don't own?' gasped Art.

" 'In this car that we don't own, yet,' I said. I told Art that if, after making love in the Volkswagen, he still didn't want to buy it, we wouldn't. I am now the proud owner of a 1997 red Volkswagen Cabriolet."

7. Open Wide

Mel and his wife, Loretta, met in dental school and now have their own separate dental practices. Whenever they need dental work, they to their favorite dentist—their spouse. Last year, Loretta needed a crown put on a tooth, so she scheduled an appointment with her husband for a Saturday afternoon.

"I like to go on Saturdays because it's a light day. Mel's office is only open half the day, and he uses one person to double as hygienist and receptionist."

On this particular Saturday, after Mel completed putting the crown on Loretta's tooth, he asked the hygienist to cover the front desk while he finished up.

"I thought it was a little strange that he would ask the hygienist to leave, but I didn't say anything," said Loretta.

"I closed the door to the examining room and lowered the back of Loretta's chair so that she was lying flat," said Mel. "When I asked if she'd like to make love, her enthusiasm shocked me. I figured she'd go along with it, but I was impressed when she moved the instrument tray out of the way, took off her napkin bib, and ran some water to muffle any noise—all in a matter of ten seconds."

"Lovemaking in a dental chair was the most exciting sex we've ever had," said Loretta. "And, because there are no locks on the examining-room doors, the possibility that the hygienist would come in at any time added to the excitement."

Since that day, Loretta's oral hygiene has become an even bigger priority than it was before. Now she sees her dentist every three months instead of twice a year.

8. Love Under the Stars

It was Darlene and Les's annual family vacation at the beach. The days were filled with swimming, sunning, and building sand castles. The evenings were usually spent sitting around playing Monopoly. After their fifth night of playing board games, the children asked if they could go exploring. "Let's all go," said Darlene. "I'd like to see the rest of the resort anyway."

As they got into the elevator, one of their kids pressed the button for the top floor. When the doors opened, they stepped out onto a huge sundeck. "Wow," said Darlene. "I didn't know this was here."

"Look how clear the stars are tonight," said Les.

After about five minutes the kids were bored with star-gazing and wanted to go back down.

"Okay," said Les. "You kids go ahead and we'll meet you at the pool in a few minutes."

Darlene gave Les a knowing look, and as soon as they heard the elevator doors close, they found a secluded corner of the sundeck, where they made love under the stars.

9. The Night We Scored

Jake and Renee had been high school sweethearts and had been looking forward eagerly to their thirtieth reunion at Oakwood High School.

"We moved away from our hometown twenty-five years ago and hadn't been back since," said Jake. "We were anxious to see the school, the teachers, and our high school friends again."

The night of the reunion, while the other alumni stayed in the cafeteria dancing and chatting, Jake and

Renee spent a lot of their evening walking the halls and reminiscing about their courting days. "Jake was a football player and I was a varsity cheerleader," said Renee. "When I suggested we go look at the football field, Jake readily agreed."

The lights on the field were off, so Jake and Renee couldn't see very much. They just sat in the bleachers, gazed out at the field and remembered their youth. "Wait," said Renee, "I think I can see the big white 'O' in the middle of the field."

"Let's take a closer look," said Jake.

Jake and Renee walked out to the middle of the "O" on the football field, where they began kissing and then making love.

Afterward, Jake looked lovingly at Renee and said, "Tonight is the most excitement I've ever had on a football field. It made me feel young and crazy-in-love all over again. Boy, those were good times, weren't they?"

10. Sex at Sea

Laurenda and Kurt are a couple of "old salts." They've both been sailing since they were children and they became sailing instructors in their early twenties. When they met in a regatta in the Caribbean and fell in love, their love for each other surpassed their love for sailing. No longer professional instructors, they still belong to a sailing club and get invited to sail with friends who have their own boats.

Laurenda and Kurt will never forget one sailing trip that gave them the opportunity to go below for some excitement.

"There were seven couples on board, and we got

under way in calm seas with lots of sun and gentle breezes," said Laurenda. "By midafternoon, the winds had kicked up and the boat was doing a lot of rolling. People were looking pretty green."

"Laurenda and I had sailed in much worse conditions and we felt fine," said Kurt. "We watched as people got sicker and sicker. When a few people tried to go below, thinking they might feel better there, Laurenda and I were quick to tell them that going below would be the worst thing they could do.

"However, for us, it was the best thing to do. Assured that no one would come near the galley, we staked out the bench seat and closed the curtain."

"We felt badly for the sick passengers, but knew that the only thing they could do was ride it out," said Laurenda. "Their misfortune turned out to be our good fortune, as we made love on the high seas."

The K.I.S.S. Plan

If the temperature of your relationship has gone from hot to cold, it's time to turn up the heat. Your romance will sizzle again if you **K**eep **I**t **S**omething **S**pecial with a quickie.

You've reached the point where you're ready for this assignment if you've put into practice all of the methods I've discussed in the preceding chapters. By now, you're feeling full of love for your partner and want to be sexually connected as often as possible. If you still feel reluctant, the next step is to practice being spontaneous in whatever way feels most comfortable to you.

Next, I want you to look around your house with a new pair of eyes. The rooms you now see as utilitarian can become places to renew your connection with each other with a quickie. Rev up each other's engines in the garage. Play with each other in your recreation room. Cook up something other than meatloaf in your kitchen.

Let the stories you've read in this chapter be the catalyst that spurs you to action. Be daring. Be spontaneous. Be sneaky and steal time from your busy life to be with your mate. The next time you get a lustful thought, pick up the phone, stop the car, meet him or her in the shower, or close that office door.

Instead of thinking, "I'd better not. This isn't a good time," or "It wouldn't be appropriate," remind yourself that now is the perfect time and this is the perfect place.

8

THE
TWO-MINUTE
BELLY LAUGH

Bust a Gut

When was the last time you and your mate laughed together? I don't mean a "tee-hee" or a chuckle. I mean a knee-slappin', side-bustin', tear-provoking laugh.

When I ask this question at my lectures, people look at me like I've asked them the answer to some complicated mathematical equation. They shrug their shoulders and get a faraway look in their eyes, as they try to remember. Someone will usually say, "I can't recall the last time my mate and I had a good laugh together."

When I ask them why they think that is, I hear about their responsibilities and obligations: earning an income, cleaning and organizing the household, paying the bills, taking care of sick relatives, fulfilling commitments at their church or synagogue, overseeing their children's educations . . . the reasons are endless.

"What's funny about my life?" I once heard a man comment.

"You'd be surprised," I replied. Suddenly, everyone's eyes were riveted on me. They were wondering how their stress-filled lives could possibly produce any laughter.

I went on to explain that our lives—yours and mine—are the inspiration for the comedians and humorists of the world. Without us, Erma Bombeck would have remained just another suburban housewife, and the only thing Jack Benny, Bob Hope, and George Burns would have had in common would have been their golf handicaps.

These immortals were funny because they saw the humor in everyday life. Situations that might induce anger or frustration in you or me could be used in a monologue by Jack Benny or a column by Erma Bombeck to entertain millions. These people gave us the gift of laughter, and we can learn how to see the humor in our lives from them.

Laughter Is Still the Best Medicine

Long before Norman Cousins wrote *Anatomy of an Illness*, in which he chronicled his recovery from a fatal disease through laughter, *Reader's Digest* knew the score. "Laughter Is the Best Medicine" has been a monthly feature in this widely circulated magazine since I was a child. Back then, we intuitively knew that laughter was good for what ailed us. Now there is ample scientific evidence to support that common-sense dictum.

Diagnosed with what doctors thought was a terminal illness, Cousins set out to find whether laughing would help relieve his pain and cure his disease. He watched funny movies, read funny books, and listened to funny stories. He found that laughing for ten minutes could give him at least two hours of pain-free sleep.

Cousins's discovery led the way for scientific research into the effects of emotions on health. This branch of science, called psychoneuroimmunology, has proven that laughing is one of the best ways to help relieve pain and heal illness.

An article in the April 1992 issue of the *Journal of the American Medical Association* provided an interesting overview of the effects humor and laughter have on your body. According to this article, laughter disrupts your normal respiration pattern and increases your breathing rate. This, in turn, increases the amount of oxygen in your blood. A good laugh also increases circulation and aids in the delivery of oxygen and nutrients to tissues throughout the body. And frequent, hearty laughter can provide limited muscle conditioning. Ever notice how your sides ache after a good laugh? That's because muscles you don't normally use have gotten a workout.

If laughter is good for our body and good for our soul, then it stands to reason that it is also good for our relationships. The couple who has learned how to laugh together has achieved a level of maturity and insight that allows them to see the big picture. When we can laugh at ourselves and our imperfections, we

prove that we love and accept ourselves as we are—
an essential requirement before we can truly love and
accept another.

Humor can even help us get through the darkest
times. Gallows humor is the trademark of people who
have to deal with death, disease, and the dark side of
life on a daily basis. Peace officers, ambulance drivers,
doctors, nurses, and mental health workers use humor as a buffer against the tragedies they witness regularly. Most of us are uneasy or even outraged by this
type of humor, but if you have the ability to see it,
there can be humor in even the most unfortunate situation.

When I was in the hospital for my bone marrow
transplant, I received scores of cards from many wonderful, caring people. Most of the cards expressed
sympathy for my condition, and although I deeply
appreciated their thoughtfulness, the funny cards
were the ones I treasured. These cards evoked my
laughter and lifted my spirits during my darkest
hours.

I also received "get well" messages by the dozens
on my answering machine at home. I'd call in every
day and listen to them, and I was always touched by
people's caring and concern. But my favorite message, the one I played over and over, was from a
friend who said, in a very matter-of-fact way, "Ellen, I
just want you to know that you're not going to die.
Only the good die young."

Another example of how humor can sustain us in
our times of hardship was shared with me by my
friend Connie. She had been undergoing chemotherapy and hadn't been out much recently. The day be-

fore she called me, she had felt better and she and her husband had decided to go to a movie.

It turned out that *Shadowlands* was not a wise choice. In it, after being married for just a short time, Debra Winger learns she has cancer and soon dies. Connie, feeling quite vulnerable began crying and couldn't stop even after the credits were over and the house lights came on.

After the movie, she and her husband went next door to a pizzeria.

When the waitress served the food, she looked at Connie's red, watery eyes and asked compassionately, "Is everything okay?" Connie looked up at her and said sadly, "This is the worst pizza I've ever had."

Connie laughed uproariously with her husband at her joke. As she laughed, she began to feel better. She put things into perspective as she reminded herself that it was only a movie; the real-life story had taken place before the advent of chemotherapy or radiation; the character did not have breast cancer, but bone cancer; and it was, after all, about somebody else's life, not hers.

Laughter changed Connie's mood from one of despair to one of lightheartedness for the rest of the evening.

Loosen Up

As adults, we often become very serious and heavy-natured in our efforts to control what goes on around us. Children don't care about control. They

live in the present moment and see life humorously
hundreds of times throughout the day. Sadly, as a
child grows older, his or her ability to laugh is seriously impaired by adults, who say "Wipe that goofy
grin off your face," "Quit acting silly," "Stop clown-
ing around," or "Grow up." I know many of you
have had laughter shamed or punished out of you, so
that the ability to see humor in everyday situations
seems to be dead. It's there, trust me. It just needs
some coaxing to come out. With a little persistence, you can overcome your learned cynicism and
reclaim your natural, innocent delight in the world
around you.

I love the following story because it demonstrates
how even the most straitlaced among us can learn to
laugh like a kid again.

One year, the night before Thanksgiving, as I dismissed the class and wished everybody a happy holiday, one of my students started to laugh. When I
asked why she was laughing, she said that since her
daughter had gotten married, Thanksgiving was her
favorite holiday. I assumed it was because her daughter prepared the meal now that she had her own
home, but Gloria said, "No. That's not the reason."
Then she explained.

"The first year my daughter was married, I hosted
Thanksgiving dinner at my house, as always. We had
a nice family group, including my new son-in-law, his
mother, and his sister. Everything was beautiful. The
table was elegantly set with my grandmother's bone
china, fresh flowers, silver candelabra, and cut-glass
goblets.

"Shortly after we sat down to dinner, I saw my

son-in-law pick up his spoon and begin rubbing it on his nose. 'What in the name of heaven is he doing?' I wondered. He placed the bowl of the spoon, ever so gently, on the tip of his nose and slowly removed his hand. Much to my surprise, the spoon remained there, dangling dangerously. He then turned his head carefully from side to side, so that everyone at the table could witness his marvelous accomplishment.

"I couldn't believe my eyes. I had never seen anyone do that before, and certainly not at a formal dinner party. While I was trying to figure out how to control the situation and regain the dignity of the occasion, I noticed my daughter pick up her spoon and attempt to dangle it from her nose. The next thing I knew, my son was following suit. Next was my husband. At this point I gave up trying to act like an adult, and broke into laughter. I laughed until my sides hurt as I picked up my own spoon and joined in the madness.

"It's become a family tradition. Now, each year on Thanksgiving, we sit down to an elegant table, laden with turkey and all the trimmings, join hands and say our prayers, and then pick up our spoons instead of our forks."

Laughter Is a Magnet

We are naturally attracted to people who are happy and laugh easily. Laughter acts like a powerful magnet, drawing those around you into your circle of influence. Nina, a woman in one of my classes, loves her job because it is a place where laughter and a sense of fun are encouraged.

"I work for a small, family-operated business," said Nina. "Many of us have been there for more than twenty years, and I'm convinced it's because we're encouraged to have fun on the job and laugh as much as we can.

"The president of the company, Mr. Goldstein, sets the tone for us. He's as playful as a little kid and he loves nothing more than a good practical joke. Every year, on April Fools' Day, the employees put their heads together to come up with a practical joke to play on the boss that will top the one we did the year before.

"My favorite April Fools' Day prank was the time the women in the office decided to put clear plastic wrap over the top of the men's toilet. We knew Mr. Goldstein's habits so we timed it perfectly.

"Nine o'clock in the morning, just like always, Mr. Goldstein walks through the door, says, 'Good morning, campers,' goes into his office, hangs up his coat, then disappears into the men's room.

"Nobody could keep a straight face. Suddenly, the door flies open, Mr. Goldstein emerges, laughing his head off, and announces, 'This means war!'

"Turning on his heel, he marches into the factory, grabs a toolbox, and makes a beeline for the ladies' room.

"Well, I wasn't going to go in there, and nobody else wanted to go in, so we all just looked at each other and waited while all this banging and clanging was going on.

"Finally the door opens, Mr. Goldstein sticks his

head out and says, 'And when I say war . . .'—then he steps out, triumphantly holding up the two toilet seats—'I mean cold war.' "

According to Nina, word has gotten out about how much fun they have, and there are never enough openings available for the number of applicants.

Laughter Is Contagious

Just like a yawn, laughter is contagious. When someone near you is laughing a natural, hearty, gut-bustin' laugh, it's nearly impossible not to laugh along with them. I have a friend who told me her favorite aunt was the world's best laugher. According to Julie, if there was an Olympic event in laughing, her aunt would have won the gold medal. Something would "tickle her funny bone," and she'd be off and running. The funniest part was, she never made a sound. The corners of her big, brown, doe-like eyes would crinkle until they were almost shut and her mouth would open in a wide smile. Pretty soon her shoulders would start to heave, then her belly would begin to shake. In no time at all, tears would be streaming down her face. She'd be laughing so hard she could hardly breathe, but if you weren't looking at her you would never know she was laughing. She was completely silent! Julie said she never saw anyone resist her laugh. When she laughed, everyone became as hysterical as she was.

"After laughing with Auntie Ruth," my friend said, "I always felt twenty pounds lighter. My sides ached, but my sinuses were clear for at least a week, and I had a spring in my step that lasted for days."

Children can do that to us, too. Whenever a toddler gets the giggles and then starts laughing uncontrollably, we catch the "laughing bug" and start laughing right along with them for no reason at all.

Sheila, a woman in one of my classes, described her nine-year-old son's laughter. "My husband and I love taking our son, Kevin, to movies. Even though the G-rated movies are often not our type of humor, we love to go just to watch Kevin laugh."

According to Sheila, Kevin throws his head back, rocks back and forth, and at least once during every movie, he falls out of his seat and into the aisle.

"Obviously, we don't give Kevin the popcorn to hold," she said.

Make Me Laugh

When I ask people what first attracted them to their mate, I frequently hear it was their sense of humor or the ability to make them laugh that was the main appeal. I remember Mickey's delight as he told me his wife stole his heart when she told him her "milkshake" story on their first date.

Toni had Mickey laughing and crying at the same time as she told him what happened when she was just ten years old and went to the Howard Johnson's all by herself.

She ordered a hamburger, french fries, and a chocolate milkshake. When the order came, the waitress set the milkshake down on a saucer, but it was a little beyond Toni's reach. As Toni pulled the saucer toward her, it hit a crack in the Formica countertop, the milkshake toppled over, and the thick, foamy chocolate rolled across the counter, over the edge, and right into her lap.

As if that wasn't embarrassing enough for a ten-year-old, the brown goop that didn't land on her shorts somehow clung to the bottom lip of the counter, running along until it reached the woman seated next to her—a woman who had made a very big mistake that morning when she'd decided to wear a white skirt.

Once the rivulet of milkshake oozed its way along the edge of the counter to a spot directly above her nice white skirt, it just seemed to give up clinging and started dropping in a steady *plop, plop, plop* as it formed a puddle of brown goop right in the middle of her lap.

Mortified, Toni babbled a hasty "I'm sorry" and fled to the ladies' room. But the lady in white must have had the same idea, because as Toni got to the door she caught a glimpse of Mrs. White Skirt headed in the same direction. Not knowing what else to say or do, Toni rushed into the ladies' room, dove behind the door of a cubicle, and hid there until she was absolutely certain no one else was in the room.

After cleaning her shorts as best she could, Toni started back to the counter. There was the lady in white, and next to her, on the counter in front of Toni's stool, was the last thing Toni wanted to see, another chocolate shake. All she wanted to do was pay and leave. She counted out her money, put it beside the glass, swiveled her stool to the left to get up to leave, and then it happened! Her right elbow hit the glass, and everything seemed to go into slow motion as the glass toppled again, the milkshake spilled again, and Mrs. White Skirt stared down at her lap in disbelief.

This time it wasn't the ladies' room. It was out the front door and down the street as fast as her legs would carry her, with echoes of "She did it again," ringing in her ears.

At the time of the incident, Toni didn't think it was very funny. But as an adult, she laughs along with her children every time she hears them say, "Mommy, tell us the milkshake story!"

The Couple That Plays Together Stays Together

Often sheer playfulness will cause us to laugh harder than a funny story ever could. In my mind, playfulness includes all of those things you might have done as a kid: snowball fights, pillow fights, tag, hide-and-seek, tickling, dancing, even wrestling. Partners who can be playful with each other have a better chance of keeping laughter in their relationship than do couples who aren't playful. Your play with your mate should be limited only by your imagination.

The best laugh I've enjoyed lately occurred when my husband and I engaged in a round of "Big-Time Wrestling," an almost annual event at our house. My husband is six foot two and weighs 210 pounds. I'm five foot six and weigh 125 pounds soaking wet. So when I told him I was going to pin him to the floor so he couldn't get up, you can imagine his terror!

I told him he needed to play by my rules. He had to lie on his back with his arms at his sides, bent at the elbows, and palms up.

"Go for it," he said.

I sat on top of him with my knees pinning his upper arms and my hands holding down his wrists. Right off the bat, I sensed he wasn't really trying that hard. So I said, "Come on, you can do better than that, you wimp!" That did it. He got serious and started to really try to lift me. So then I got serious and tried harder to hold him down, grimacing with the strain.

When he saw the determined look on my face, he knew he was in a war. He started straining himself and that started me laughing. He let out a loud grunt, which made me laugh even harder. Then, with a burst of energy, he was able to turn me over and get on top of me. By now we were both laughing hysterically, wrapped in each other's arms, rolling on the floor.

That little wrestling match remains very vivid in my memory. Life can be so serious so much of the time. I figure by letting go of stress and playing like children, we probably added at least a couple of weeks to our lives and to our relationship.

I also laughed when I received the following letter from a man who sounded like he had the ability to use playfulness as a way to keep laughter in his relationship:

Dear Ellen,
Light His Fire *and* Light Her Fire *were just what I was looking for to get my marriage of twenty-six years out of the pits.*

You said you like to collect stories, so here's how I tried to be less predictable and boring.

My wife and I had just returned from the Bay Area, where we watched sailboats and visited gift shops as part of a mini-vacation. When we got home, my wife worked on her students' report cards, while I decorated the living room using a sea-faring theme. I put a blue sheet over the windows to ensure privacy and represent the blue sky. I put a beach towel filled with sailboat designs on a mattress I hauled from the bedroom, and I lit scented candles nearby. Then I took off my clothes, hung three Ping-Pong balls by a string from my you-know-what, and presented myself to my wife saying, "You're right. I really am oversexed." Her laughter filled the room, and we pretended we were on board a sailing yacht on the bay at night, just the captain and his first mate, alone under the stars. I proceeded to give her a long massage with scented oil and was very well rewarded for my efforts.

Our do-it-only-in-the-bedroom routine turned into an imaginary voyage that has burned a memory into our minds forever.

Sincerely, Captain on Board (used to be bored)

Just Foolin' Around

Many times we get ourselves into a situation that will keep us and our children laughing for generations to come. One of the funniest stories I think I've ever heard about playfulness was told to me by Suzanne.

Suzanne's children loved it when she and her husband, Murray, played hide-and-seek with them. During one particular game, Suzanne dumped all the toys out of her son's big plastic football-shaped toy box and hid in it.

"It was a great hiding place," said Suzanne. "Nobody could find me until I popped my head out the top and yelled *surprise!*

"I had managed to squeeze my shoulders and torso up through the hole of the toy box, but that's as far as I got. I was stuck. There I sat, like a jack-in-the-box, with the top of my body sticking out of a plastic football.

"Murray and the kids were rolling on the floor laughing. I was laughing too, until I realized I really couldn't get out of the thing. Murray and the kids pushed the football over on its side, thinking I could wriggle out of it, but my hips were wedged in and no matter how hard I tried, they wouldn't budge. Murray pulled my arms while the kids pulled the toy box, but all that did was hurt. Five minutes had gone by and I was still stuck.

"Suddenly there was a knock at the door, and I saw our neighbor through the window. 'Oh, this is great,' I thought. 'Just what I need is an audience.'

"Now Murray is laughing, the kids are laughing, and our neighbor thinks it's hilarious. I'm not laughing anymore. 'Who do you call to get a woman out of a football,' I asked in desperation.

"The best we could come up with was the fire department, who laughed right along with everyone else as they sawed me out of the football. In the background, I heard Murray answering phone calls from the other neighbors and telling them, 'No, Suzanne doesn't do parties.' ''

The Joke's on You

A practical joke can be a good source of laughter, if it's done in good taste. A practical joke played on your mate that carries the underlying message "I love you" will be welcomed with a sense of fun. By catching your mate off-guard or surprising him or her with an unusual gift, you are reminding your mate that he or she is on your mind. On the other hand, a practical joke is not funny when:

- The laughter is the result of an insult.
- The laughter stems from sarcasm.
- You laugh at your mate instead of with your mate.
- You embarrass your mate by revealing something told in confidence.

The following stories are both good examples of practical jokes done in a loving way.

After reading *Light Her Fire,* Scott decided to play a loving joke on his wife, Bobbie, as a way to keep himself in her thoughts for the day.

Bobbie took their two kids to the grocery store one afternoon. The store was packed with shoppers stocking up for the long Labor Day weekend ahead. After twenty minutes of standing in line, Bobbie finally unloaded the items in her grocery cart onto the conveyor belt.

"I'll never forget what happened when it came time for me to pay," said Bobbie. "When I opened my change purse, out popped Scott's bikini underwear. I watched in shock as it landed on the conveyor belt and moved toward the cashier between the chicken and the Ty-D-Bol.

'In a voice loud enough for everyone to hear, my daughter asked, 'Mommy, why are we buying Daddy's underwear?' The cashier looked at me wide-eyed as I grabbed my husband's underpants and shoved them back in my purse. 'Don't ask,' I said, as she opened her mouth to speak.

"I thought of Scott all day and we both laughed until our sides ached when I told him where his underpants had been that day."

Roberta and her husband, Nathan, got a lot of laughs from a practical joke she played on him one morning.

"There is a lingerie and sex-toy shop in our city," said Roberta. "Every time I passed the store, I'd see these blowup dolls for sale. I always thought it would be funny to buy one for Nathan and surprise him with it somehow as a joke."

Roberta told me that a few months ago, she bought the doll and blew it up one morning while Nathan was in the bathroom showering for work. "I was laughing so hard while I was blowing it up, I almost didn't get it inflated in time," said Roberta. "I ran down to the garage and propped the doll up in the driver's seat of his car, then ran upstairs just as Nathan was walking out of the bathroom."

"I remember that morning very clearly," said Nathan. "I had an important meeting with a client and I was running late."

When he was done getting dressed and eating his breakfast, Roberta kissed him good-bye at the back door to the garage. She watched him walk to his car, open the door, and stare in surprise at the blowup doll.

Nathan started to laugh, but realized he didn't have time for shenanigans, so he pulled the doll out of the car and tried to deflate it.

"I was doubled over with laughter as I watched Nathan try to deflate the doll. He squeezed it, folded it, and even stomped on it to get the air out. For the life of me, I don't know why he didn't just leave it on the garage floor. When I saw him prop the doll up next to him in the passenger's seat and drive away, I thought my bladder was going to give way."

"I knew Roberta was watching me," said Nathan, "so I put on a little show to make her laugh. Just so you know, I stopped the car and threw the doll in the trunk at the first stop sign I came to."

How Do You Spell Relief?

Laughter not only releases tension in our bodies, it can be very effective in relieving tension between mates. Kyle's zany sense of humor diffused a huge argument between him and his wife, Kendra, and created a memory both of them often laugh about.

"It was a Sunday morning," said Kendra. "As usual, we were running late for church, and there was a lot of tension in our household. Our kids were upstairs getting dressed, and Kyle and I were arguing about something in the kitchen. I can't even remember what we were arguing about," said Kendra. "I just remember getting angrier and angrier. Somewhere in the back of my mind, I knew it was over something stupid, but I was on a roll and didn't know how to stop."

"I could see we were going nowhere," said Kyle. "So I did something to put a halt to the whole discussion. Pretty confident that the kids wouldn't come downstairs, I peeled off my sweatshirt and sweatpants, and stood there completely naked, except for my white athletic socks."

"I totally cracked up," said Kendra. "Kyle looked so silly and vulnerable wearing nothing but his socks, that I went over and gave him a great big hug. We were both laughing uncontrollably.

"Within five minutes, neither of us could remember what we had been arguing about, but we were still laughing hours later. In fact, we had to seat the kids between us in church to keep ourselves from giggling during the service."

A Funny Thing Happened on the Way to the Jetway

Some of our funniest memories come from a time when our mate has done something completely out of character. When we do something that deviates from our normal behavior, our partner is caught by surprise and his or her reaction is intensified. Those crazy memories can keep us laughing for the rest of our lives together.

One of my "out of character" moments happened when I had to pick up my husband from the airport after he had been gone on a five-day business trip.

I had not felt very sexy since my diagnosis of breast cancer, but this day was different. I had missed him a lot while he was gone, and the anticipation of being with him again motivated me to get out the red light bulbs for the bedroom lamps and prepare for his homecoming with love in mind.

In a daring mood, I decided to go to the airport dressed in a raincoat and nothing else. The traffic was heavier than I had expected, so I was cutting it close. With little time to spare, I parked the car and rushed toward the gate so he could see me as soon as he arrived.

"Oh God, no," I thought. I was next in line to go through the metal detector and I had completely forgotten about my porta-cath. Now, a porta-cath is not something you put in those little baskets along with your car keys and loose change. A porta-cath is a metal device that is implanted surgically to help the doctors administer drugs. Mine had been in since my chemotherapy treatments.

It was too late to back out because I had already put my purse on the conveyor belt, and I'd have to go through the metal detector to get it.

I thought I was going to die! In that split second, I pictured the sound of the metal detector going off, and me passing out on the spot. Worse yet, I pictured me not passing out, the security guards asking me to remove my coat, me refusing, and a combination of the F.B.I., a S.W.A.T. team, and the bomb squad surrounding me. My naked body was a surprise I had planned for my husband's eyes only, not the Los Angeles police department or the National Guard.

Fortunately, I didn't make the metal detector go off, but I was as white as a ghost and could hardly catch my breath. After spotting my husband, I finally composed myself enough to give him a kiss hello. Then I immediately burst into laughter as I told him what had just happened.

We were both still laughing hysterically as I painted another catastrophic picture for him. My mother had always told me to wear clean underwear, so that if I were ever in an accident I wouldn't embarrass myself in front of the ambulance drivers or medical staff. My husband and I could not stop laughing as we wondered what the doctors and nurses would think if a woman wearing a raincoat and no underwear were to arrive in their emergency room on a stretcher.

Life's Embarrassing Moments

Aside from making us feel like we want to crawl into a hole and never come out, being caught in the act of being human can be a wonderful source of laughter. In the early days of TV there was a show called *Candid Camera* that did just that. A hidden camera was used to film people in embarrassing situations, and it was one of my favorite shows. Today's answer to that show is *America's Funniest Home Videos*, one of the most popular shows on TV. We're all human beings who make mistakes and blunders. Laughing at our own embarrassing predicaments makes us just as lovable as we are vulnerable.

Sherrie and her husband, Hal, laugh whenever they remember one of Sherrie's most embarrassing moments. "We were at the twenty-fifth anniversary celebration of Marriage Encounter," said Sherrie. It was a formal affair for two hundred people with a sit-down dinner and a dance band. It was held at a popular hotel in Los Angeles.

"A priest named Father Ed was the after-dinner speaker. Although I couldn't see him very well because we were seated at a table in the back of the room, I was very impressed with his talk, and wanted to tell him so. After dinner, I turned to Hal and said, 'I'll have to make sure to find Father Ed later and tell him what a great talk he gave.'

"Later in the evening, I saw Father Ed and went over to him to compliment him on a speech well done. I approached him, touched his arm, and said, 'Hi, I'm Sherrie. I just want to tell you what a great speaker you are.' He looked at me quizzically and said, 'Oh, why, thank you. Where have you heard me speak?' Feeling the blood rising up my neck, I asked, 'Aren't you Father Ed?' 'No,' said the priest. 'I'm Father Rick.' Crimson-faced, I mumbled something like, 'Oh, I'm sure if I had heard you speak, I would have loved it,' and hurried away.

"I found Hal and told him how I had humiliated myself, and we both chuckled at my blunder. About half an hour later, Hal pointed to a priest about twenty feet away and said, 'Look! There's Father Ed!' In my zeal to tell him what a wonderful orator he was, I ran over to him, put my hand on his arm, and said, 'Hi! I'm Sherrie. I just wanted to tell you what a great speaker you are.'

"As the last two words came out of my mouth, I realized that this priest looked familiar. He looked at me as if I needed a lobotomy and said, 'I'm Father Rick.'

"I burst out laughing, babbled something about not having had anything to drink, and stumbled away. I found Hal, who had witnessed the whole scene, leaning against a wall convulsed with laughter.

" 'You knew that was Father Rick, didn't you,' I said, still laughing. Hal, now with tears running down his face, nodded his head yes.

" 'How could you send me over there knowing it wasn't Father Ed?' I asked. 'I was kidding you when I said, "Look, there's Father Ed," ' said Hal. 'But you were off and running before I could stop you.'

"By the time Hal and I peeled ourselves off the wall, the party was over, and so was my career as a seminary recruiter."

I don't know why, but airports seem to be the setting for many of life's embarrassing moments. Elise's moment came when she and her husband were in the Newark, New Jersey, airport, on their way home from a week in Jamaica, where they had celebrated their tenth wedding anniversary.

"It was during the Persian Gulf War, so security in the airport was very tight," said Elise. "I remember standing in line waiting for our bags to go through customs when one of the security people looked at me and said, 'Excuse me, miss, would you step over here for a minute.'

"As I saw which bag he had held aside, I began to sweat profusely. Inside the bag was my vibrator, which probably looked like a gun in the X-ray machine.

"When I glanced over at Roger I noticed he was rubbing the back of his neck nervously, and looking at the ceiling.

"The young security guard opened up my suitcase, looked at my vibrator, and asked, 'What's that?' I took a deep breath and said, 'How old are you?' He looked a little surprised at my question and answered, 'Twenty-one.' I took another deep breath and said, 'That, young man, is a vibrator.'

"Then, to my extreme embarrassment, he held up my vibrator like the Statue of Liberty, and yelled across the room to another young security guard, 'Hey Mike, I wish my girlfriend would get one of these!'

"Mortified that every person in line for customs now knew my sexual habits, I muttered urgently, 'Just put it back in the suitcase, would you, please?'

"Then I turned to my husband and said, 'I'll be in the bathroom for the next few years,' and I headed straight to the ladies' room to wait for the thirty-five people in line behind us to get through customs."

Lighten Up

If we lighten up a little, we'll find that there are a lot of opportunities to laugh at simple things in our day-to-day lives. Most of what we encounter during the day is not that serious, but somehow we make it that way.

A friend of mine told me a story that illustrates perfectly some people's inability to laugh when the opportunity presents itself. Her eleven-year-old son loved gags and pranks and was forever looking for new ideas at novelty shops and in catalogs.

For his birthday, she bought him a box full of gags. Included was a big metal nail that he could wear on his head so that it appeared as if the nail was penetrating his skull.

"One afternoon my son went to the hardware store with me," said my friend. "I didn't know it, but he had brought along his nail. When we went up to the counter to make our purchase, I tried to keep a straight face as Johnny approached the clerk with this huge nail going through his head and said, 'Excuse me sir, can you tell me where you keep the pliers?'

"I couldn't believe it when the salesclerk looked my son straight in the eye and said, 'Pliers are in aisle seven.' How could the clerk have missed the fact that my son had a nail stuck in his head?"

It was a shame the clerk had so much on his mind that he missed a simple opportunity for laughter.

You Had to Be There

The purpose of this chapter is to remind you of the importance of keeping laughter and fun in your relationship. The stories were included to help you remember the times in your life when you laughed helplessly with your mate and to induce you to lighten up and take advantage of the opportunity to laugh as often as possible.

Obviously, I'm not a comedy writer. While these stories made me laugh when they were told to me, it's very difficult to put them down on paper and have them be as funny as they were when I heard them. Without the body language, the laughter in the narrator's voice, and all the other nuances that are part of a good story, chances are a lot has been lost in the translation. My only hope is that the stories served to spark a memory of times when laughter brought you and your mate closer together and to reawaken you to the joys of laughter you experienced as a child.

The K.I.S.S. Plan

Sharing the joy of laughter can strengthen and deepen your relationship with your mate. **Keep It Something Special** by incorporating laughter into your relationship on a daily basis.

Whether you're alone or with your mate, look for reasons to laugh. Even if you find yourself laughing alone, share the story with your mate later. If you laughed, chances are your mate will too.

Laugh at yourself. Remember, life is not as serious as we make it out to be. Make light of your shortcomings. We all have them. Write down some of your funny stories so you won't forget them.

Play with your mate. Play games, playact, play house. I don't care what you play, just play! Enjoy the freedom of acting silly and knowing that no one will tell you to grow up. And if they do, who cares!

Last of all, lighten up. Learn to look at life as if you were looking through the lens of a video camera. Taking a long-range view can help you put things in focus. I'm here to tell you that no matter what happens in your life, although it may seem awful at the moment, there will come a time when you can find a reason to laugh about it.

To laugh easily is truly a gift. If you have it, use it. If you don't, learn it.

9

THE
TWENTY-FOUR
HOUR DAY

Two Ways of Living

There are twenty-four hours in any given day. Every day of our life begins with 86,400 seconds to do with as we choose. We can either fritter away our time, spending our moments foolishly as if they were just so much loose change, or we can realize that each moment we spend adds up to the net worth of our entire life. How we spend our life is determined by how we spend each moment, and how we spend each precious moment is our choice.

I believe that we can choose to live our lives one of two ways. We can either live our life coming from a fearful place, or we can live our life coming from a loving place.

Let me explain.

Deep down inside every human being is a place where nothing exists but love. It is in this place that we are connected to everyone and everything. It is the place where we are pure, whole, and unafraid. It is the place where we know that we are perfect, just as we are, and that whatever actions we take—*from this place*—are right. When I talk about coming from a loving place or coming from a loving state in this chapter, this is the place I'm talking about. This place is our core, our essence, our soul. And in this place we have the wisdom and the insight to always choose the right action.

Also within all of us is fear. Some of our fears are obvious to us: fear of heights, fear of pain, fear of water. But a lot of our fears are more subtle. We've learned to cover up our fear, ignore it, deny it. Fear is often disguised in socially acceptable ways. For example, a person who is overly agreeable (otherwise known as the doormat) may be motivated by fear of rejection. The community volunteer (otherwise known as the do-gooder) is often motivated by fear of not being liked. The head of the company (otherwise known as the high achiever) might be motivated by fear of failure.

Seldom is fear so blatant that we experience the classic physical symptoms, such as sweaty palms, racing heart, and rapid breathing. It's usually far more deceptive and, in the long run, far more destructive than the outright terror we might experience if our life were threatened in some way.

If you've never thought about it before, I want you to become aware of how you live your life. Do you live it in fear, always playing it safe? Or do you live it in love, knowing that you are worthy and trusting yourself and your loved ones? Realistically, none of us is totally free of fear. It's normal, even healthy, to feel fear. But to live in a way that supports our lives and the lives of our loved ones—in fact, that supports the world in general—we must be aware of when we are acting out of fear instead of love. And being aware, we must work to come from love more, and from fear less.

In my own life, I have been happiest when my decisions were made from love. I started teaching my courses on relationships out of pure love. I had discovered techniques and ways to relate to my husband that worked for me and I believed I could help other people put fun, romance, excitement, and communication into their relationships as well. I was going to provide a valuable service and it was unimportant to me whether or not I earned money from this endeavor. I was always willing to stay after class or come early if someone needed to talk to me privately about a problem they were having. If someone wanted to tape my class, I made sure they had a seat up front so they could record the lesson. Sometimes it was for their own use, but frequently it was for a friend or relative who lived too far away to attend the class and wanted to make sure they got the information straight from the source. Because I came from a loving place, my only goal was to impart as much information to as many people as possible.

If I had come from fear, my decisions would have been quite different. I would not have allowed my lessons to be taped, fearing that they would be used to cheat me out of tuition money, or that someone would use the tapes to teach the classes themselves. Not only would I have not allowed it, I would have become angry at the person making the request, feeling ripped off when in actuality nothing had happened.

I'm so glad that I came from a loving place, without even knowing that there was another way. It was so much fun teaching the classes and my students knew that I had their best interests at heart.

It feels so much better when we make a choice based on love instead of fear. Even if your decision turns out to be a big mistake, I believe that you'll never be sorry. When someone says, "Maybe it was a mistake, but if I had to do it over again, I'd do the same thing," they are referring to a decision they made from a loving place.

When I began my book tour I didn't care about how many copies were sold, or which bestseller list I made. In fact, when my publisher called to congratulate me on making the *New York Times* bestseller list, I asked, "Is that good?" I thought to myself, "I'd prefer to be on a California list, since that's where I live." I had no idea that the *New York Times* list was the most prestigious of lists and the one every author dreams of achieving.

As I became more successful, my attitude began to change. I thought of myself as the *New York Times* best-selling author of *Light His Fire*. Now there was pressure to do even better with my next book, *Light Her Fire*. I was concerned with the results. I cared about how many books were being sold. I cared about the money I was getting paid, which was never enough. Negotiations that used to take a day, now took weeks to finalize. I hired lawyers to protect me from being cheated out of any money. Life became a series of annoyances and frustrations.

I'd get upset at not having enough TV or radio airtime. I didn't want to appear on just one or two segments; I wanted the whole show to revolve around me. Eventually I became more demanding and difficult to deal with. I had gotten a taste of fame and fortune, and I wanted more.

Then came the wake-up call named cancer. My life was on the line. My career suddenly became unimportant, as I mustered all of my strength and resources to fight my disease. Too sick to continue the rat race, I had a lot of time to reflect on my life. I saw that a shift had taken place in recent years. What started out as a labor of love had become a prison of fear. I was afraid of not receiving enough recognition. I was afraid of not getting enough money. I was afraid of not selling enough books. I was afraid I was not spending enough time with my husband and children.

The truth was that everything in my life was out of balance. I was staggering under the weight of the stress I had created for myself. After much soul-searching, I came to realize that I had been living my life based on fear. I was financially successful, but I wasn't having nearly as much fun as I'd had in the beginning.

I knew I had to change the way I was living. I knew my life depended on finding a balance among my body, mind, and spirit. To do that, I had to constantly monitor my decisions and examine my motivations. I had to be vigilant—not for attack from others, but for sabotage from within. Greed, arrogance, and mistrust—all fear-based qualities—had to be replaced with gratitude, humility, and trust.

My journey from utter chaos to a place where love exists again was long and arduous, but it was worth it. Pursuing my career has become fun again. I no longer worry about money or fame. For me, success means helping as many people as I can. I'm closer to my family than I've ever been and I have wonderful friends that I will cherish forever. Professionally, I'm surrounded by good people who are dedicated and honest and have integrity. I feel a constant flow of love between myself and the world, and life is good once again.

I begin each day with prayer. And every day I pray for the ability to make my choices based on love. Every evening I give myself a grade. Some days I do better than others. But I can tell you this: I always know when I've missed the mark, because what happens in my life reflects my inner state of being. When I'm living my life based on love, things seem to flow naturally and I'm a much happier person.

Fearful Thoughts Cause Fearful Feelings

How we perceive a situation controls our response to it. Two situations can be exactly the same, yet one person will experience fear while another one doesn't. For example, if you were faced by a large dog that had just escaped from a yard surrounded by a chain-link fence, you would feel fear. Your brain would signal danger and your body would automatically go into a "flight or fight" response. Your adrenaline would flow, causing your heart to pound and your muscles to tense. Your conscious thoughts might be, "I'm going to be attacked," or "That dog is going to take a chunk out of me and the pain will be unbearable."

On the other hand, if you had prior acquaintance with this dog and knew it to be sweet and docile, you would feel quite differently. You might think, "How did he get out?" or "I need to get him back to his owner." You would feel no fear and have no physical symptoms. You would feel calm and unruffled.

As another example, a camping trip can be something to look forward to or something to dread, depending on your thoughts about it. If it brings up visions of huge black bears, snakes, and other "creepy-crawlies," dirt and discomfort, a camping trip could be something to avoid at all costs. If, on the other hand, it evokes thoughts of sitting by the fire, roasting marshmallows, taking long walks, and sleeping under the stars, a camping trip would be something to anticipate with pleasure.

I remember a day trip my husband and I took from Hong Kong to China. On our return to Hong Kong, we had to go through customs. We were on a long line that was moving fairly quickly. My husband went through without a hitch. When it was my turn, I smiled and handed the customs officer my passport, expecting him to give it a quick glance and nod his approval, as I had seen him do for the people in front of me.

Instead, he looked at my passport, gave me an uncomfortable stare, and motioned for a guard, who commenced a detailed search of my purse. I broke out in a cold sweat and I found it difficult to breathe as my heat started racing. In the brief time that this procedure took place, I developed an entire screenplay in my mind. I pictured myself screaming, "Help, help, I'm innocent! I didn't do it!" as the guard hauled me off to jail. Maybe someone had put something illegal in my purse. It could have been drugs or even a bomb. In either case, I would never see my husband and children again. As these thoughts raced through my mind, I heard the customs officer say, "Next, please."

If I had been told before I went through customs that every fifth person would be searched a little more thoroughly, my reaction would have been completely different. I would have stayed calm and unworried as I realized that I was going through a routine search. Instead, I experienced fear and anxiety because of my thoughts. The truth was, I was afraid of traveling to a foreign country. I had heard stories of people being falsely accused, convicted of a crime they hadn't committed, and prevented from leaving that country. With no one to turn to for representation, they would end up in jail for years. Since I'd had these thoughts prior to going through customs, the slightest glitch triggered a fearful response.

Handling Fear

By being aware that how we view events controls our response to them, we can begin to change our perceptions. Most of us formed our views based on what we learned as children. Because our parents were all-powerful and all-knowing in our eyes, we believed what they told us without question. Without being conscious of it, we automatically adopted our parents' view of life as our own. Since most people are driven by fear, in all likelihood your parents' lives were fear-based, and that is the way you live your life today. As adults, we have the opportunity to choose a different way. By looking at things differently, we can change how we react to them.

To live your life in a fearful state is to rob yourself of pleasure and new experiences. More importantly, when you live in fear it is impossible to experience a deep connection with others, including your mate. But there is a way to handle your fears that can increase your awareness and put them in perspective. Whatever you fear, whether it's rejection, failure, the unknown, or criticism, there is an effective way to handle it.

I believe that the harder you try not to think about something, the more it will obsess you. So the next time you are afraid, don't fight it. In fact, I want you to imagine the worst-case scenario in vivid detail. Carry out the situation to the worst possible conclusion. Then, when you're done, ask yourself these two questions:

- Are these thoughts destructive or supportive?
- Are these thoughts coming from a loving place or fearful place?

If your thoughts are destructive and are coming from a fearful place, I want you to take a few deep breaths, to calm down and give yourself a sense of well-being. Then I want you to create a new picture of what you would like to have happen instead.

I remember being scared to death as I waited for my turn to appear as a guest on *The Oprah Winfrey Show*. I couldn't have been more scared if a robber was threatening me at gunpoint. The interesting thing about fear is that our physical response is the same, regardless of whether it is our ego or our physical being that is threatened. There was no robber threatening my life, only Oprah and her live audience, but my body didn't know the difference. My heart was racing, I was sweating, and my hands were shaking. After all, she could destroy my credibility.

I gave myself up to the fear and pictured the worst-case scenario.

I was afraid that I would make a fool of myself on national TV. I pictured Oprah asking me a question to which I wouldn't know the answer. Oprah would shout to her producer, "Who booked this guest?" and the entire audience would start laughing. I would slowly walk off the stage, beet red, wanting to crawl into a hole. My career would be over. I would slink home in shame because everyone I knew had seen my humiliation.

When I was done with my catastrophic story, I took a deep breath and asked myself, Are these thoughts supportive? The answer was no. Are they coming from a loving place? Again, the answer was no. So I changed my thoughts and pictured myself as the perfect guest. I answered every question with ease. Oprah, as well as her entire audience, nodded in agreement with whatever I said. With these supportive thoughts I was able to walk onto the stage with confidence. By the way, my supportive thoughts turned out to be quite accurate. It was a great show and a wonderful experience.

I've used this same exercise many times before getting on an airplane. Prior to my first publicity tour I hadn't done much flying. The little I had done was always with my husband. When I learned that I had to fly from one city to another every day for two weeks, I was anxious. I began to imagine the worst-case scenario. Intellectually, I knew that I was safer flying in a plane than driving in a car, but I couldn't stop myself from getting fearful and thinking about the plane crashing. To keep myself calm, I'd take a few deep breaths and picture the smooth ride, the wonderful service, and the enjoyable conversation I'd have with the person sitting next to me. I'd visualize the perfect landing and imagine leaving the plane with a smile on my face. With these more supportive thoughts, I was able to board the plane.

Jenny, a woman in one of my lectures, was able to use this technique in a similar way. She had recently been promoted to the position of western regional sales manager for her company. She was responsible for a large territory and would be doing a great deal of driving. The first time Jenny was faced with driving a long distance, she started to panic. She remembered what I'd told her, and didn't fight her fear. Instead, she began to picture the worst-case scenario. She might run out of gas. Her car might get a flat tire or break down in the middle of nowhere and she would die from lack of food and water. Or she'd be robbed and beaten by an opportunistic thug. Jenny realized that her thoughts were destructive and coming from a fearful place. She knew that if she continued with them, she could not do her job. So Jenny took some deep breaths, as she had been coached to do, and pictured a perfect trip. She visualized interesting scenery, the sound of beautiful music filling the car, and a feeling of freedom as she cruised the highway, away from the interruption of jangling phones. Her ability to visualize the desired outcome enabled her to drive without fear.

Fear in Relationships

In a committed relationship, the decisions you and your mate make will guide your life together. Whether it's deciding to buy a house, have a baby, or change careers, your decisions will affect the dynamics of your relationship. If you make your decisions based on fear, your relationship will be haunted by insecurities, anxiety, and negative energy. If you make your decisions based on love, your relationship will be touched by nothing but warmth, confidence, and trust.

If you experience difficulty making a particular decision, there is probably some kind of fear involved. To make the best decision possible, use the following steps. First, ask yourself, "What am I afraid of?" It could be fear of losing money, fear that you can't make it on your own, fear that you won't succeed, fear that you'll disappoint someone, fear that you won't be loved anymore, or fear of losing someone you love. So first, I really want you to face what you are afraid of.

Next, I want you to ask yourself, "If I were coming from that loving place deep inside, if I knew I was completely safe, that my instincts were trustworthy and my motives were pure, how would I react and what would I say or do?" The answer to this question is sometimes very different than what you would normally do or say, but it will be the right answer.

I've helped many people by using this technique. One of them was Monica, who came to class very distraught one night. She told me that her husband had come home from work the day before and proudly announced that his company was doubling his salary, making him vice president of a new bank, and moving his family from California to Arizona.

Monica said that all she could think about was how lonely she would be if she had to leave her friends and family behind. She couldn't imagine coping with her nine-month-old baby without the help of her mother. She knew no one in Arizona and didn't make friends easily. She had cried all night, and in the morning she had told Peter she didn't want to go. Peter had left for work without speaking. They still hadn't spoken when she came to class that evening.

I asked Monica to picture the worst-case scenario, including all of her fears. She did a pretty good job of it. She pictured herself crying every day as she sat by herself in her lonely house with the baby screaming. She felt isolated, depressed, and angry.

I asked her if these thoughts were supportive and coming from a loving place.

She said, "No, and they are making me miserable."

I asked her to pretend that she was coming from a

loving place, a place where she was safe and secure and all of her thoughts were supportive. Then I asked her what she would do or say if that's how she felt. She looked at me as if I were crazy and said, "But I don't feel safe and secure. I'm scared."

I said, "I know that, but if you were coming from a loving place instead of a fearful place, what would you do? Just for a moment, pretend."

Monica said, "Well, if I felt safe and secure, then I would be excited about going. I would tell my husband how proud I am of him and what a wonderful opportunity this would be for us. If I weren't scared, I'd be excited about buying our first home because the prices are so much lower in Arizona than they are in California."

I did everything I could to convince Monica that she should make her decision from that loving place where faith prevails and not from a fearful place. I'm happy to report that Monica and Peter did move to Arizona; later, she sent me a note letting me know that she'd joined a "Mommy and Me" swim class and had made some wonderful new friends. They bought a home in a good neighborhood, and the lovely retired couple who live next door are delighted to help out with baby-sitting.

If Monica had made her decision based on fear, she never would have stepped out of her comfort zone and experienced a new adventure, and her relationship would have been damaged, if not destroyed completely.

Another student told me she and her husband were struggling with a financial decision. "If only we had a crystal ball, this decision would be so much easier to make," she lamented.

"Well, none of us has a crystal ball," I replied, "so tell me what the problem is and let's see how we can solve it."

Darlene proceeded to describe the situation to me. She and her husband, Gary, were recently retired and living on a fixed income. They found it necessary to cut their living expenses and had leased their town house to a reliable couple at a good price. As an alternative, they had decided to live in their mountain cabin, which was paid for. The cabin was old and rundown and much too small to be comfortable, however. The decision Gary and Darlene were struggling with was whether or not to spend the money, a substantial sum, to remodel the cabin and make it more livable.

I asked Darlene to imagine the worst-case scenario. Boy, could that woman catastrophize!

"Okay. We borrow the money to remodel the cabin. Gary dies and my income is cut in half. I don't have enough money to repay the loan, and I lose the cabin. I can't afford to live in the town house, so I sell it, but I take a tremendous loss because the real estate market has hit rock bottom. I get sick, can't work, and end up using a shopping cart for a closet and living in parks."

When she had finished, I told Darlene to take a couple of nice, deep breaths and to picture the outcome she wanted. She did that equally well.

"We get a great loan at a ridiculously low interest rate, find a wonderful contractor who understands our needs and is a perfectionist, Gary and I have a ball discussing the different options and solving the problems that come up, I get to buy that antique sink I've been eyeing because it'll fit perfectly in the remodeled bathroom, and we receive unexpected income to help repay the loan."

Next I asked Darlene what she would do if she were to let go of all her fears and make her decision coming from a loving place, where she was safe and secure.

"I'd have faith that everything would be fine, and I'd start looking into loans and interviewing contractors," Darlene responded. She and Gary did decide to go ahead with the remodeling and, strangely enough, things have worked out pretty much as Darlene visualized them.

I recall helping a man named Ned grapple with a dilemma he was caught up in. Ned explained that he had spent the last few nights arguing with his girlfriend about whether he should attend her ten-year high school reunion. She had asked him to go with her, but he had turned her down. He thought it was a waste of time and money. He'd have to pay airfare, spend fifty dollars for the reunion itself (for a ten-dollar meal, he added), have a few drinks, talk to people he didn't know, pay for a motel room, and then go home the next day. She had said it would be fun, but he knew better. Even if she had a good time, he would just feel like an outsider. She was being selfish, not thinking about him at all.

When I asked the class if Ned was coming from love or fear, everyone said he was coming from fear. Ned was shocked and disagreed. He said he wasn't fearful. He just thought his girlfriend's idea was stupid.

It took a while for Ned to finally see that he was afraid of losing his girlfriend. He worried that after a fun-filled weekend with her classmates, she might decide that he was just too quiet and not enough fun to be around. He was also threatened by the fact that she would be seeing several ex-boyfriends and he wouldn't be able to compete with them. When he finally recognized his fear, I asked him what he would do if he were coming from a loving place. He said that if this was so important to her, then the loving thing to do would be to go with her. He knew that she loved him and that she had never given him any reason to be jealous. The money wasn't really an issue, it was just a smoke screen.

I heard from Ned after they came back from the reunion. He said they had so much fun that they planned to go to her next reunion as husband and wife.

Fear of Being Less Than Perfect

Many people let their poor body image keep them from happiness. We've all been exposed to such unrealistic ideals of the human form and face that it takes a superhuman effort to overcome the fear of being less than perfect. Perfect faces and perfect bodies are everywhere we look. Magazines, TV, movies all glorify perfectly sculptured faces and hard bodies. It's nice if you happen to be beautiful, but it's certainly not necessary for a happy relationship. If it were, only the beauties we see on screen would have relationships. The old sayings "Beauty is only skin-deep" and "Pretty is as pretty does" are as true today as they were in our grandmothers' day.

As we get older, many of us fear that we will no longer be physically attractive to our mates. After all, we reason, how could someone love our wrinkles, flabby skin, and aging bodies? The truth is, love doesn't fade as we age. In fact, it's just the opposite. When you really love someone, you love that person from the inside out. His or her internal beauty increases and deepens with age. Every line, wrinkle, and stretch mark represents the precious time you've been together and the memories you've shared. By accepting your body with all its flaws, you accept yourself.

We could all learn a valuable lesson from Bonnie, a woman I met at one of my cancer support groups. She had recently had a mastectomy, and although her physical recovery was complete, she said that emotionally she felt scarred. She told me that she no longer felt sexy and her husband, Leonard, was acting differently toward her. She revealed that Leonard no longer looked at her when she was getting undressed. Most of the time he stayed out of the bedroom until she was in bed and safely under the covers. He also avoided touching and hugging her. She told me that they used to enjoy kissing and holding each other close, but now it seemed that his kisses were performed out of obligation and felt very superficial. There was absolutely no body contact at all.

"Obviously he finds me repulsive," Bonnie wept. "We no longer have a sex life, and to tell you the truth, I don't blame him. Why would any man want a woman who wasn't complete?"

After comforting her, I asked Bonnie to try an experiment. I wanted her to pretend that she was the most sensual, loving, grateful, seductive woman alive. She was to become an incredible actress. "That's crazy," she responded. "I can't do that looking and feeling the way I do now."

"Please try," I said. "I know you're afraid of being rejected because you don't feel physically attractive. I want you to find out for yourself that it's not true. You are never going to feel differently unless you take a chance and behave differently. I want you to ask yourself, 'How would I act if I was completely safe, and coming from a very secure, protected, and loving place? What would I do or say differently?' I know what I'm asking you to do is scary, but living the way you are now is scarier."

When I saw Bonnie again a few weeks later, she looked radiant. When I asked her if she had done what I'd suggested, she laughed and said, "How wrong I've been. I'm so glad that I took your advice." She then proceeded to give me some of the details.

"I prepared a special dinner, served it with wine, soft music, and candlelight, and after dinner I asked Leonard to sit next to me on the couch. I turned to him and said, 'Please darling, hold me. I really need to feel your arms around me. I've missed you so much. I miss feeling your body close to mine.'

"When he didn't respond immediately, my heart sank. Then I heard him say, 'But I'm afraid of holding you because I don't want to hurt you.' "

Leonard cried as he told Bonnie how he had tried

to comfort her a few weeks after her surgery. When he had tried hugging her, she'd winced with pain and asked him to stop. He had not realized that the incision would be so tender. He said he felt like a brute and certainly didn't want to cause her more pain. He had decided that he wouldn't touch her or try to caress her again until she told him it was all right.

That was why he didn't kiss her passionately anymore and why he stayed on his side of the bed, rather than cuddling with her like he used to. The reason he never looked at her while she was undressing, he confided, was because he didn't want to embarrass her.

"I'd gotten everything completely backwards," Bonnie told me. "I wanted to believe he loved me, but it was very difficult because I felt so maimed. I wanted to be close to him and was so hurt when he turned away. It never occurred to me that he was afraid of hurting me.

"I'm so glad you encouraged me. When I think of the torment we went through, I realize that we both wasted a lot of precious time."

If anything, Leonard's love for Bonnie had deepened because of her surgery, not diminished.

Fear of Not Measuring Up

Many people have a fear of inadequacy and are constantly struggling to live up to what they believe others expect of them. What they fail to understand is that no matter how hard they try, they will never get the approval they seek. When we live our life based on love instead of fear, we don't need to be approved of by others in order to feel safe and secure. Our own approval is enough. When we focus on fulfilling the expectation of others and ignore our own needs, we are ignoring a basic rule of survival. I remember one of my students who found this out the hard way.

Stephen, whose father was a physician, was expected to follow suit. When Stephen decided to become a carpenter instead, his father withdrew his love and approval.

Stephen spent many years trying to prove himself to his father and win back his love. Shortly after he got married, Stephen took on a major remodeling project. He excelled at his work, and other projects soon followed.

"When I started building custom bookcases, mantels, and staircases for million-dollar homes, I was sure my father would be impressed, but I still got no approval from him," said Stephen.

In addition to the custom carpentry he was doing, Stephen began working forty hours a week for a contracting company. He was now working an average of seventy hours a week.

"I knew I was pushing too hard," said Stephen, "but I couldn't stop."

Two years after they were married, Stephen and his wife, Cheryl, had a son.

"I felt like a single mom," said Cheryl. "I teach full-time at an inner-city high school. Between caring for the baby, teaching, and Stephen's insane work schedule, I was close to having a nervous breakdown. Our marriage was really suffering and I was seriously thinking of leaving Stephen."

A few months later, Cheryl's stress level rose another couple of notches when Stephen's employer closed down the contracting company and her father died of a heart attack . . . both on the same day. Instead of viewing the job loss as an opportunity to slow down, Stephen filled his windfall of time with more subcontracting work until he was back to working seventy hours a week. "I didn't want my father to think I had failed," said Stephen.

It was while remodeling the unoccupied side of their duplex home that Stephen got the wake-up call that saved his marriage. Stephen had already worked ten hours as a subcontractor when he came home at five o'clock to grab a quick dinner and cut the lawn before going next door to work on the duplex. By ten o'clock that night Stephen was exhausted and pushing himself to finish a strip of molding for the dining-room ceiling. As he lined up his miter saw to cut a notch in the wood, he was overcome with fatigue.

Although he thought he had a firm grip on the saw, Stephen will never forget watching as it jumped an inch off-center and severed the thumb from his left hand. Stephen scooped up his thumb and screamed for Cheryl.

"It wasn't even a scream," said Cheryl. "It was more of a yelp. I couldn't imagine what was wrong until I opened the door and saw Stephen standing in a puddle of blood." Stephen spent the next few hours in surgery having his thumb reattached.

"Once my thumb was reconnected, I decided it was time for Cheryl and me to do the same," said Stephen. "I had always been fearful of not living up to my father's expectations. But after the accident, I vowed to live my life in a loving way by accepting myself for who I am."

Whenever Stephen starts to worry about what his father thinks of him, he simply glances at his left thumb to remind himself that he doesn't need anyone's approval but his own.

Fear of Saying the Wrong Thing

Sometimes we avoid or distance ourselves from someone who has experienced a death, loss, or illness for fear of saying the wrong thing, or of not knowing what to say. We don't want to embarrass ourselves, so we stay away.

Matt told me he did just that when his girlfriend's mother passed away. "I didn't know what to say to make her feel better, so I left her alone," said Matt. "A couple of weeks later, she broke up with me because she said I wasn't there for her when she needed me."

Matt admitted he had been afraid of saying the wrong thing.

When I asked him what he would have done if he had come from love and not fear, he immediately said, "I would have been with her, held her and hugged her, and let her know how much I cared."

Somewhere deep inside we know the loving thing we'd do if we could just let go of our fear and trust ourselves.

Fear of Taking a Risk

Another student regretted not taking advantage of an opportunity to invest in his own business. Chris had a decent job and a steady income and was always able to pay his bills. He had learned early in life to "pay himself first," so he saved whatever he could out of each paycheck, but he worried that it would never be enough to take care of his and his wife's needs in retirement.

At one point, Chris and Bette had an opportunity to buy an ice-cream shop.

"I saw the ice-cream shop as a real chance to build for our retirement," said Bette. "I was excited about going into business with Chris, but he didn't want to risk the chance of losing our savings. So, we decided against it."

"All that I had saved would have been used to get us started in the business," said Chris. "It had taken us so many years to save a few thousand dollars that I couldn't stand the fear of losing it all."

Chris's fear of not having enough money to retire kept him from making an investment in his future. His fear was a self-fulfilling prophecy. He didn't invest, his money didn't grow, and he didn't have enough money to retire. If Chris had been able to trust in his own instincts, he would have found a way to earn more money. He would have been confident in his and his wife's ability to make the ice-cream shop a success, or he would have read, taken classes, and gotten some advice on investing wisely. Instead of creating the circumstances he feared, he would have created the circumstances he desired.

The Choice Is Ours

When we live in a fearful state and all our actions support fear, that which we fear is likely to be manifested.

When we live in a loving state and all our actions support love, that which we desire is likely to be manifested.

Let's look at some fearful thoughts, the actions that support them, and the results. Then we'll look at the loving thoughts, the actions that support them, and the results.

> **Fearful thought:** I'm afraid to leave my dead-end job.
> **Fearful action:** You never spend the energy to network and interview.
> **Fearful result:** You stay in a job where you feel unfulfilled and underpaid.

> **Loving thought:** I will find a way to explore new job opportunities.
> **Loving action:** You network, make a resumé, and interview for several positions.
> **Loving result:** You land a job with more growth potential and more income.

> **Fearful thought:** My mate will leave me.
> **Fearful action:** You act insecure by becoming jealous and needy.
> **Fearful result:** Desperation is such a big turn-off that eventually your mate leaves you.

Loving thought: I want our love to last forever.

Loving action: You treat your mate with kindness and respect.

Loving result: You mate loves being with you.

Fearful thought: People will find out that I'm not smart enough.

Fearful action: You never give your opinion or disagree with anyone. You don't take any classes to improve yourself.

Fearful result: You stagnate and reinforce your opinion of yourself.

Loving thought: There's so much I need to learn.

Loving action: You continue your education, engage in discussions, and ask questions.

Loving result: You grow and develop more interests.

Fearful thought: I hate going to parties with my mate. I'm afraid I won't know anyone and I'll feel alone and left out.

Fearful action: You never go to a party with your mate. Eventually your mate goes without you.

Fearful result: You feel alone and left out.

Loving thought: It's okay to meet new people.

Loving action: You go to parties even though you don't know anyone at first.

Loving result: You meet new people and you and your mate make new friends.

I'm sure you can add many more fears to the above list. Everyone has fears. No one is immune to them. We can either exercise control over our fears and take action in a loving state or we can live in a fearful state and risk ruining our precious relationships.

Your fear will always get in the way of having a healthy loving relationship. To be fearful in a relationship means to isolate, defend, guard, protect, and take whenever you can. To be loving in a relationship means to risk, expose, be accessible, be vulnerable, and give whenever you can.

The choice of whether to live in fear or love is yours to make every single day of your life. Either state is a self-fulfilling prophecy, meaning that I will get what I expect; therefore I choose to live the rest of my life making every decision based on love. I know that if you, too, choose love over fear, your life will be more rewarding and fulfilling than you ever dreamed possible.

Gratitude

The key to living in a loving state is to be grateful for what we have. Most of us take life for granted and fail to appreciate the gifts we've been given. The next time you feel a little down, I want you to take a few minutes to think about how miraculous your life is and experience the gratitude that witnessing a miracle produces.

■ Are you breathing on your own? There are people at this moment who need a respirator to help them breathe.

- When you got up this morning, were you able to hear the alarm go off? Could you hear the birds singing, the wind blowing, the heat or air-conditioning going on? There are people who are deaf and can't do that.

- Are you able to talk? Can you scream, whisper, or sing a song? There are people who will never be able to use their vocal cords.

- Look around you. Can you see the clouds, the blue sky, the grass, and the flowers and the trees? There are people who see only darkness. They are blind and cannot see nature's beauty.

- How about your legs? Can you walk, skip, jump, hop, and crawl? There are people who are confined to a wheelchair for the rest of their lives.

- Did you have enough money to buy food today? Most of the world doesn't have welfare, food stamps, or social security. In fact, one-third of the people in the world will go to bed hungry tonight.

- Do you have a home to live in? All over the world, there are men, women, and children who are homeless.

- Do you have bills to pay? That means that someone was willing to trust you enough to give you a product or service in advance of getting paid. There are many people who have no credit and cannot get anything without cash in their hands.

- Do you have a savings account? That means you were able to put some extra money away for a rainy day. There are so many people who don't have enough money to get through today.

Just think how lucky you are to be able to use your lips for kissing, your arms for hugging, your ears for listening, your voice for talking, and your body for making love.

The K.I.S.S. Plan

Your relationship is a blessing. **Keep It Something Special** by acknowledging your gratitude each and every day.

This is your last assignment. I want you to reflect on your life and the decisions you've made. What was your reason for getting married, having children, moving, taking a different job, buying a new home? Have the decisions you've made come from a fearful place or a loving place?

Look at the decisions you are faced with today. Ask yourself, "Are my thoughts supportive and coming from a loving place or destructive and coming from a fearful place?" When fearful thoughts come up, remember, don't fight them. Go ahead and play out the worst-case scenario. Then take a few deep breaths and create a new picture of what you want to have happen instead.

I have learned that fear paralyzes and love energizes. Whenever you feel overwhelmed by fear or negative thoughts, reread the section on gratitude. When you learn to be grateful for what you have instead of fearful and angry about what you don't have, living from a loving place will come naturally to you.

For the next twenty-four hours, choose to live from a loving place. I know if you do, you'll continue living this way for the rest of your life.

CONCLUSION

No Regrets

At the time I started writing this book, I had just completed a new infomercial. The production company traveled the United States interviewing people who had listened to my audiocassette programs. They were chosen because of the letters they had written to me about the incredible changes that had taken place in their lives as a result of my tape programs. Two weeks after the infomercial was filmed, I received a letter from Harriet, who had appeared in the show with her warm, loving husband. Imagine my sorrow when I read the following:

I am sorry to inform you that my husband died suddenly this past March 11th from heart failure.

I want you to know that I will be forever grateful for your wisdom. The information we learned helped us share partnerships, priorities, passions, and romance in a dimension we had never known before. Your program had a lifestyle-changing revelation for both my husband and myself.

We have known each other since the third grade, and have been married for thirty-four years. There has never been anyone else in our lives, and yet we felt our relationship had come out of a dark musty cellar, and into the light of a warm summer day.

I will miss the joy of his smile, his gentle love and the warmth and safety of his embrace. I will always cherish the love we shared and the memories we created together for each other, over the last five months, because of your program. He gave me enough love to last a lifetime.

Thank you for sharing your gift of teaching love and romance with those of us in need.

With a grateful heart—THANK YOU.

Harriet gave me permission to print her letter with the hope that people who read it will realize that the time to make things better is now. We just don't know how much time we have together.

The Bottom Line

Some of you have not followed any of the K.I.S.S. Plans at the end of the chapters. Perhaps you've told yourself that you're too tired, too busy, too nervous, too overweight, too old, or too scared to do the assignments. You say that you'll try some of these things next week, next month, next year. We always think we have tomorrow. In fact, some of you live your life according to Mark Twain's quip, "Never put off till tomorrow what you can do the day after to-morrow." Listen to me when I say, Do not put your relationship on hold for another minute. The truth is that the person you love may not have tomorrow.

One of the coping skills that has always kept me going is that I've always had a bottom line. Whenever things got out of hand and I became overwrought, I'd say to myself, "Look, Ellen, the bottom line is, this is not a life-and-death situation, so just calm down!" It worked very well most of the time. It certainly worked when I tried to potty-train my kids too early, had a disagreement with a neighbor, or had a dead-line to meet.

When I was diagnosed with breast cancer, my bot-tom line was suddenly pulled out from under me and rendered useless. This was a life-and-death situation. I no longer had a bottom line, and I was in a state of panic.

As I learned to live with my disease, I discovered a new bottom line: No one knows if they will have to-morrow. I used to think that people who died unex-pectedly from a heart attack or an accident were lucky to die instantly. I don't think so anymore.

Now when I hear about someone killed in a car accident or a plane crash or murdered in a senseless crime, I wonder what they would have said and done differently in the last two years, the last two days, or even the last two hours, if they had known with abso-lute certainty that their life was going to end on that particular day.

I wish I could give you the same sense of urgency that I feel. You do not know how much time you have left to love your mate the way he or she deserves to be loved. Don't let another day go by without putting into action the K.I.S.S. Plan presented here:

- Kiss for at least ten seconds—every day.
- Compliment at least one thing your mate has said or done—every day.
- Talk and listen to each other for thirty minutes—every day.
- Hug for twenty seconds—every day.
- Stay connected sexually.
- Plan a fantasy for each other.
- Make love on the spur of the moment.
- Laugh together—every day.
- Make all your decisions based on love.

We are here for such a short time that it is imperative to make that time count. Don't live a life filled with regrets. Love like there's no tomorrow, because in the end love is the only thing that counts.

Printed in the United States
by Baker & Taylor Publisher Services